GET HAPPY
and Create a
Kick-Butt Life!

GET HAPPY
and Create a
Kick-Butt Life!

A Creative Toolbox to Rapidly
Activate the Life You Desire

JACKIE RUKA

NEW YORK

Get Happy and Create a Kick-Butt Life
A Creative Toolbox to Rapidly Activate the Life You Desire

Tele-classes by Jackie Ruka
Create the Life You Want 6 week Program

OM - Operation Miracles Year long Program

Gross Domestic Happiness Assessment: www.gethappyguide.com

Happiness in Life and Business
Workbook: A Course in Reinvention

Inspirational Posters available at: http://society6.com/JackieRuka

Meet Jackie online and receive free life enhancement techniques at:
www.gethappyzone.com

Published in New York, New York, by Morgan James Publishing. Morgan James and The Entrepreneurial Publisher are trademarks of Morgan James, LLC.
www.MorganJamesPublishing.com

The Morgan James Speakers Group can bring authors to your live event. For more information or to book an event visit The Morgan James Speakers Group at
www.TheMorganJamesSpeakersGroup.com.

ISBN # 9781630472405 paperback
ISBN # 9781630472412 eBook
ISBN # 9781630472429 CB

Cover Design by:
Jackie Rukie with graphics by Shaila Abdullah

Interior Design by:
Shaila Abdullah: www.myhouseofdesign.com

Dedication

I CONTINUE TO FEEL DEEP GRATITUDE FOR THE BEAUTY OF LIFE that surrounds me every day regardless of the hurdles endured to improve the quality of my life and especially my physical well-being. Had it not been for the lessons learned, the skills and talents that God graced me, life would not be nearly as colorful. Even when self-doubt creeps in, it has been faith in knowing that God and my special angels surround me with love and guidance. The Universe truly has my back.

This book is dedicated to my father, William Ruka. I find him whispering to me, "Do what makes you happy." I miss my best friend everyday but feel blessed to have had him as long as we did. I lift my glass to you while you enjoy the dance floor of the heavens above.

To Mom, Chrissy, and Dylan, I love you. I am so proud of you and thank you for your support, friendship, love and laughs. Thank you for caring so passionately for our family, Mom. You have a heart of gold and you will always be loved and taken care of.

To my close friends who have lifted me up and been here for me no matter what. Thank you for your lifelong friendship and support, love you much: Marcie George, Carolyn A. Brent, Alexis Guerrier, Richard Romero, Jeff and Michelle Mattson, Jer and Mariella Swain, Joy Liu, and Cheryl D'Angelo.

This book would not be possible without the talents, assistance and dedication by editors; Stephanie Gunning, Teri Breier, Ray Estrada and Nina Gass. My appreciation of the artistic talents of Shaila Abdullah, Sean Kirkpatrick, Albert Mandile and Lucinda Kinch.

Thank you to all the wonderful women and men for the support on all the social media sites including Facebook fans and friends. I feel privileged to my students, clients and friends who have allowed me to share their case studies and stories in this book.

Contents

List of Illustrations

Suggestions to Readers

Dear Reader,

THANK YOU FOR ALLOWING ME TO SHARE WITH YOU that which I know and teach. This book incorporates life enhancement tools and ideas to implement, as part of your new toolbox, to grow and heal within your life and live your dreams out loud.

Nothing is as powerful as the human spirit, for it unifies us as one. As you proceed on your growth path towards emotional freedom, you become happier and you can create a happier world. And despite what is occurring around us, it is each person's inner world where the work must begin. During challenging times, getting down to the basics and simplifying our lives creates a greater flow of abundance in areas of your well-being encompassing career, social, physical, financial and your community well-being. A stress-free lifestyle, where you are doing what you love and feeling fulfilled, is integral in your quest for getting more out of life.

I created this book as if you and I were collaborating to create your true heart's desires. If you do the exercises progressively, as they appear in the book, you will begin to change your life for the better. You will feel challenged and inspired mentally, visually and creatively, where you utilize and exercise the whole brain, stimulating a consciousness for you to organically reach positivity.

For support, you may want to share the exercises with a friend, support group or family member.

Each chapter incorporates life enhancement techniques that are pivotal to overcoming obstacles in that area of your life. The final section of the book offers inspiration and imagination to stir your soul's purpose. Should you require a mantra to fuel positivity, in a particular area of your life, please turn to the last chapter of moxie mantras. Take a few days with each chapter and utilize the mantras each morning when you awaken and just before you go to sleep as part of your new practice to re-train your brain and develop the life you are meant to live.

I share with you my awakening in the Introduction. I hope it will show you that no matter what occurs in our lives, each lesson has a blessing behind it, and we can develop lives with more meaning during each step of our respective journeys.

Put all you have into each section and you will get a hundred fold back. Know that you have my loving support as the star that you truly are.

To your happiness,

Jackie

Introduction

WE ARE ALL HERE TO BE HAPPY AND LEARN unconditional LOVE!!!

During our life paths, we all experience small and large instances of feeling challenged, vulnerable, and unprepared. I term the more significant of these episodes as RUDEwakenings. This is when you experience a profound change in your life that interrupts the sleeping cat within and can, frankly, turn your world upside down.

Why do these things happen? Typically, it is an outer force, God, or your personal guide that has a higher purpose in store for you. Perhaps a current part of your life has reached its term. Every one of us has at least one major life change that gives us no choice but to pick up and rebuild, reinvent, reorganize and, my personal favorite, RENEW! When change and your RUDEwakening occurs, your world seemingly has one, two, or even three layers that ripple and fall away, leaving you raw and alone.

Perhaps you:

- Lost your job and home or lost a parent or loved one
- Are going through divorce and/or a financial loss
- Have experienced an unprecedented health issue
- Feel unable to align with your life's purpose or personal niche
- Or, find yourself starting over and rebuilding at a time in your life when you expected to be settled down

My own multi-layered collapse lasted almost two years. It began the day that my car careened out of control. As the car slowed down to a final stop, it actually landed between not one, but two eight-foot Buddha statues. The universe was trying to tell me to slow down and take a good, hard look at my life.

As I lay flat for almost six months, recovering from back trauma and dealing with the pain that comes with several other long-term debilitations, I had no choice but to walk away from a six-figure career to rescue my own well-being. When faced with our own mortality, human beings truly begin to understand how much we take our lives for granted.

My life had changed in an instant. One moment I was crazy busy, always running with barely any time at home as I scurried around to please everyone else. The next moment was an MRI scan followed by endless physical therapy, doctor visits, and trips to the pharmacy. Ceaseless pain was my companion every day, as was the ominous scrutiny of an insurance company that believed everyone commits fraud, including me.

After the accident, my world lacked any familiarity and I lacked any type of enthusiasm. It took all I had to crawl out from underneath the covers and I was unable to function without pain. I was in a perpetual state of unhappiness. As a self-help and healthcare professional, I was stunned to be in a place where my body and my life were crumbling around me and I was unable to stop it. Had I just turned into a poster child for the chronically fatigued and emotionally exhausted? This does not happen to me, I thought. Yet from these feelings that came from this experience that has led to the toolbox I have created and now teach. It contains my own emotional recipes and "soul-utions" designed to claim personal growth and become fearless. To heal and cope with initial positive challenges, I found the place to start the rebuilding process:

Whatever you are seeking is seeking you. A good way to remember this is by turning ON your BOLD. B.O.L.D. = Believing Opens Life's Dreams.It is action that encourages breakthroughs. This is a no-matter-what attitude combined with the knowledge that you will keep moving forward. The process of moving forward, mentally and physically sparks a forward attitude on an emotional and spiritual level.

We are much stronger than we give ourselves credit for. Your RUDEwakenings are confirmation of your will and determination where possibility lies. There is always a window that opens when a door shuts in our lives.We have the power to turn those RUDEwakenings into AHA-wakenings!

Negativity. Self-Doubt. Fear. These strong emotions don't have to overtake your outlook. The truth always surfaces — and that truth is we are born to WIN! Like mine, your collapse could be calling in disguise.

It's a time when your unique destiny is ready to emerge. The old must fall away so the new can enter. That is often when we experience.

Unfortunately, when tragedy hits our lives and loss occurs, it is a painful experience and redefines our perception of gratitude. I have learned that with loss, you begin from believing in miracles to relying on miracles. And soon, impossibilities become possibilities of fulfillment that you can't begin to fathom. The AHA moment brings us face-to-face with this conscious choice: Would you rather walk through life, kissing butt and waiting for something good to happen, or would you prefer to be kicking butt by creating and claiming your true heart's desire?

By awakening to our own consciousness, we recognize that life is not happening to us; life is responding to our "vibrational" energy. It is a time to reclaim your own happiness and live with fierce moxie (a term denoting determination and where the fearful become fearless). It will be your positive vibration that attracts the world to you. When you survive major change, you must be willing to live out and to your full potential and dream bigger than you ever have before. You must make a conscious effort to overcome your fear and become fearless to turn your dreams into a reality. Will there be discomfort? Absolutely! This is how you know you are living. Part of the dream is the stretch beyond the limitation of self, as we know it.

Through counseling clients, as well as my own experience, I have learned that usually, it's when life throws you a curve ball that you are being asked whether or not you are growing. Denial is an "unconscious bubble" that makes many of us complacent like a cat that chases its own tail. Author Wayne Dyer tells it like this: The cat believes that its tail represents happiness and, therefore, continuously grabs and tugs at it. Conversely, a cat that is flowing forward in life realizes its tail of happiness is always there, connected, and following right behind. Are you a cat that is chasing your tail, yet still ending up in the same spot with an unsatisfying result? Then maybe it's time to shift that paradigm so you start understanding that your "happiness tail" is always connected to you. The best method to move forward is an unrelenting belief in self.

Statistics from CNN state that 85 percent of Americans are unhappy in their jobs and 75 percent of people suffer unknowingly from chronic stress. You may be questioning what your role is during these times as well as how happiness and fulfillment fits into all of this fast-paced change.

In part, this is a time for healing our lives, our world, and ourselves. The healing process has us considering what we truly desire that will make our hearts sing and motivate us to reach our highest potential. The more we recognize that we are each responsible for our own happiness, the closer we are to seeing that our happiness powers the path to improved relationships, careers, finances, and health, as well as assists with other issues and areas of life.

To recognize how powerful your happiness can be, we simply need to adopt a new mindset by activating the following steps:

Follow Your JOY – It may not feel like it, but your joy exists within you and it is a clear path to what your heart truly desires. When you are listening and acting upon your joy, your ego does not communicate "I can't, shoulda, woulda," thoughts and destructive self-talk excuses behind your feelings of unworthiness. These feelings become non-existent when you place zero energy behind your ego thoughts. When you "Just Own Yourself (JOY)," you become the CEO of YOU and fall in love with expressing your MOXIE.

Ignite Imagination - Give yourself permission to imagine what your life looks and feels like beyond what it is now. It's ok — even great — to daydream. Just BE and ALLOW yourself to have some fun with your own psyche. By doing so, you unlock the keys to the treasure within and let go of any obstacles standing in your way. Imagine the emotional or physical pain you have been suffering with is now part of your past, and no longer exists. Even if this is just a brief respite that lasts a few minutes, it is a relief to your mind and body that you can feel good and pain free, one step at a time. You are being guided by your imagination when you begin to feel and recognize the endless possibilities within and around your world.

Deliberate Creation – This is the conscious, intentional focus of marrying your desired intention with vision, and strategically acting in your external world where you co-create with Spirit to manifest an outcome. As you collaborate with your inner creator by putting action behind positive intent and matching your positive feeling with positive action, you become an unstoppable magnet for the continuous flow of positive change. Creativity is a component of the life force for all that we do. Your ability to create remains infinite through choice. From the moment you rise in the morning, you create your thoughts, your day, how you present yourself to the world and the quality of your life. Decision making is the number-one trait that supports being the champion of your life. When you choose to tap into the positive life forces within, you intensify your vibration and become a force of power beyond your imagination.

Have a Cup of Courage – Your dream is usually outside of your comfort zone. It takes courage to walk a new path you have not navigated before. Have a cup of courage a day. Sip-by-sip, your vision is sharper and your dream becomes attainable. Courage is a more productive avenue when you reverse the energies of your fear.

Live with Conscious Happiness – This is the ability to deliberately change an old perspective with a new, positive action. Choosing happiness every day in today's complex world is not just a choice; it's a lifestyle. By re-training the brain, you can develop this new power practice. Decades of research relate the choice toward happiness to improving your health, increasing blood flow to the brain, and encouraging an enhanced ability to make decisions. When your mind and body feel good, you become spiritually in sync with your divine purpose, and your life becomes more meaningful and authentic.

Employ Creative Tools – These tools become the catalyst for making change here and now. Many people believe that change occurs with our thoughts alone. However, change may not happen even after years of psychotherapy and insightful epiphanies — although you may end up with more clarity and focus about where you are today in relation to your past. What encourages change, here and now, are tools that propel you into your future rather than analyze your past. Throughout the pages of this book, you will discover these life enhancement tools that can steer you around obstacles, crystallize your uniqueness, and direct you toward a satisfying future.

Reinvent an Authentic Self – The path to reinvention is a straight one from head to heart although it may be long and arduous. As you become your ultimate other or higher self, the spiritual spark that keeps you on track with your life's purpose and in touch your joy and passion - listening to our truth while simultaneously acting upon it may seem like peeling an onion while holding back the tears. Saying good-bye to your ego is a process of letting go of superficial attachments or illusions. Most will only dig when they know there is pure gold; you must be willing to do the work since that gold lies within your heart. Through thoughtful diligence, you can then continue on the route to happiness because the gold has revealed your authentic power. When we live in our truth, we can change the world in fascinating and magnanimous ways.

Tools spark insight and ignite action. During my RUDEwakening, as I stepped into unknown territory, I imagined being both a pathfinder and a path maker. My old life was falling away and I was blazing a trail toward a dream and imagined legacy... How does one do this, you may wonder, as I have done during such unsettling times? It's usually when experiencing breakdowns that breakthroughs appear. This is how I developed the tools for the creative toolbox — I have used these tools myself and they work!

It is my experience that every soul on this earth has a light in them. The light in some are brighter than others. There are souls whose light may be dim or darkened by trauma. At times, we allow our own light to be tamped or outshined by someone we think we love. Other times, we may choose to take a back seat in life for others, a restrictive belief, or a chemical substance. Often, we are even frightened by our own light and how brightly it can shine. Although we may stumble and fall, our light still remains; it's a matter of choosing how to re-ignite your light and the direction in which to shine it.

This is precisely why it is imperative to take advantage of all your senses and brainpower. You never know what will spark your idealism into realism. Throughout this book, there are messages, pictures, quotes, tools and some writing exercises to stimulate both the right and left hemispheres of your brain and invigorate the endorphins that are waiting to be ignited and stimulated.

Life is not based on how you compare to others; it is far more fulfilling to reach your highest potential. When you identify and harness a unique quality within yourself and have the moxie to express it in a way only you can, you have not only enhanced your life, but you have also added to the lives of others. By giving rise to your inner light and voice, you share your gift and re-birth your essence. This, in itself, sustains your powerful, sacred happiness. You may be one step from greatness, one product away from wealth, one soft word from love and one step toward your true calling and passion. Let's imagine, let's play, let's be true to ourselves and let's enhance our lives together. It took me many years to learn this perhaps because I am a late bloomer in certain areas of my life. This is OK. We are all blooming as part of the process of healing and growing.

My calling is to add some extra sunshine, water, nurturing, and food for thought. When you practice conscious happiness, you enhance your progress, manifest your desires, and take your life beyond kick-butt to kick-ass!!

To your happiness,
Jackie

1

the Happiness *revolution*

"Your vision will become clear only when you can look into your own heart. Who looks outside, dreams; who looks inside, awakes."
—Carl Jung

The Power of Your Life Force

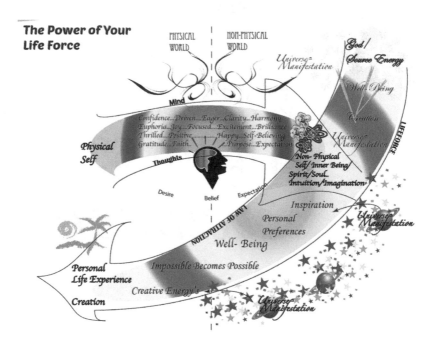

PHYSICAL WORLD | NON-PHYSICAL WORLD

Universe=Manifestation

God / Source Energy

Well- Being

Creation

Universe= Manifestation

LIFEFORCE

Mind

Confidence...Driven....Eager...Clarity...Harmony
Euphoria...Joy....Focused....Excitement...Brilliance
Thrilled....Positive..............Happy...Self-Believing
Gratitude...Faith.........................Purpose...Expectation

Physical Self

Thoughts

Non- Physical Self/ Inner Being
Spirit/Soul...
Intuition/Imagination

Desire   Belief   Expectation

LAW OF ATTRACTION

Inspiration

Personal Preferences

Well- Being

Impossible Becomes Possible

Universe= Manifestation

Personal Life Experience

Creation

Creative Energy's

Universe= Manifestation

CHAPTER 1

Welcome to the Conscious Party

> "There has always been a longing in the human heart for a more just, free, loving and creative society. But it was never before possible to fulfill these aspirations, because we had neither the evolutionary drivers and global crises to force us to change, nor did we have the scientific and technological powers that can free us from the limitations of scarcity, poverty, disease, and ignorance. This is the time of awakening for the social potential movement."
> – BARBARA MARX HUBBARD

YOU'RE OFFICIALLY INVITED TO THE CONSCIOUS PARTY! Who doesn't like a party, right? This is no ordinary party though — no costumes, masks, or facades allowed. Just you, showing up in all your glory! It's been said that 90 percent of succeeding is showing up! We are all experiencing a transformational awakening together. What is so cool about this is that it gives us all a second chance to be who we really want to be, do what we truly desire, and live with our hearts and minds open.

Have you heard of the term, tabula rasa? The Latin term means "blank slate" and according to Webster's Dictionary, it is defined as "something existing in its original pristine state." The mind is in its hypothetical primary blank or empty state before receiving outside impressions. By re-training the brain, I believe that we have the power for this to occur at any time. By abiding by our true nature, our minds become clear, and our brilliance unfolds as we rediscover the intelligence of our essence. It is a type of rebirth where you get to start again with this clear mind.

It may be hard to grasp what a clear mind actually feels like without taking a long, relaxing vacation away from personal issues and the complexities of today's world. You want to find clarity — but what will it take for you to grasp what a clear mind feels like?

Conscious Happiness

Remember Cindy Lou Who from "The Grinch Who Stole Christmas?" by Dr. Seuss. She was the bright-eyed, little girl and the hero of the story. A timid child, she displayed the most profound courage of anyone (including adults) in the city of Whoville. She represented and reclaimed what she and all the Whos of Whoville most loved, the happiest feeling known to its inhabitants: the feeling of Christmas.

Benefits of Practicing Conscious Happiness:

All feelings are fleeting.

Your Well-Being is reinforced by feelings of fulfillment and joy translated in our brains.

Compassion becomes a form of controlled emotional response, away from the negative, replaced by loving kindness.

Increased awareness equates to start each and every day with what you want to create, not what stops you.

Cindy faced up to the meanest, greediest, most self-absorbed creature — the Grinch — who was slowly stealing and hiding the happiness of each inhabitant until there was no happiness left. The Grinch believed that stealing every trinket, toy and piece of tinsel that symbolized happiness would leave an emptiness that the Grinch was all too familiar with: misery. As the snow began falling in Whoville, all the Whos gathered and sang joyous songs despite not having any symbols of their happiness.

Cindy Lou represented the conscious happiness of the story, and the Grinch represented the false belief of perceived happiness. When the symbols were eliminated, the Grinch believed his response would be satisfaction. However, the true response was emptiness, a projection of the Grinch's deep insecurity. The conscious happiness, however, is what prevailed. You see, what you might believe represents your happiness is a misperception or illusion. When you elevate your consciousness, you begin to see what truly is fulfilling to you. You can still create your own happiness, but it lies beyond your familiar perceived mindset.

In recent history, society has sought instant gratification. This collective consciousness has instilled what we believe is happiness but that is really a false sense of entitlement along with a mistaken sense of happiness. In reality, we all have the capacity to live happily when we follow our individual truth and don't look for instant results.

Each of us was born with a "barometer of happiness." It's our task to regulate this internal barometer so we can feel 100 percent happy more often than not. It will take a new belief system and conscious intention. We are all here to learn unconditional love where happiness is not only a lifestyle — it's a conscious party!

Are We in a Happiness Revolution?

"Revolution" can be defined as a significant and dramatic turnaround. Throughout human history, revolutions have varied widely from political to military to social upheavals. Many revolutions that have occurred outside of the political sphere are recognized as having transformed society, culture, philosophy, and technology. The social and technological changes happen at a breakneck speed these days — and whether or not you are a "tech geek", an ardent social media participant, or stay-at-home mom, we are affected by major life changes.

Whenever dramatic change occurs, the hardwired reaction in our brains to stress is a fight-or-flight mode, guided by the two universal feelings of fear and love. The harmony of what we think, what we say, and how we act is one pathway toward happiness. However, this is based on the decisions you make — you can choose your feelings, actions, and conclusions.

Unfortunately, most individuals act from fear, which is an ego-based default mode. Decisions are often put on hold and left for "someday." Some believe they are unable to do it alone or will be more successful if they lose those next 10 pounds, have more money in the bank, or meet the perfect mate before making a change that will enhance their lives.

Ask anyone on the street what it is that they most want in their lives and the majority will say, "To be happy!" Decades of research concludes that a sense of happiness makes us productive, improves our health and leads to stronger relationships, which builds morale. Most recently we've seen society's morale wither when faced with economic, personal and social challenges, but this, in itself, is part of the cycle that occurs in fashion, finance and the economy. Unfortunately, we are a society that tends to look externally for answers as opposed to within. Therefore, we rely on an external barometer to determine our moods and way of life, which does not seem to yield the desired solution. Here's why:

One of my career avenues led to consulting with organizations to define and market their brands, a few of which launched into blockbuster billion-dollar franchises. Surrounded by thought leaders and masterminds in the healthcare industry, I learned what it takes to navigate to the top of the heap and the pressures behind reaching a lofty goal. When obstacles lay ahead, the only choice is to change lanes or, in some cases, blazing a whole new trail. The number one mindset in working with a successful team is that failure is not an option. This often entails major commitment and a willingness to make personal sacrifices. Such sacrifices can affect your personal well-being, home life, and relationships, leading to an out-of-balance life. For example, I could have chosen to stay under the covers and allow my life to go by or go back to a career that almost killed me. At the time, I believed there was one of two paths to choose; however, I chose a new road, and new life emerged for me.

One should not work so hard to make a living that he or she misses out on creating a life. Yet, research shows that 85 percent of Americans are unhappy in their current jobs (CNN Money Magazine Survey 2011). According to the World Health Organization, one out of three Americans is diagnosed with depression, and more than 75 percent suffer from chronic stress and are completely unaware of it. This does not account for the percentage of unemployed who are struggling to find their place and offer their talents. The "failure is not an option" mode is an old belief system based upon fear and competition that results in working too much (now known as "workaholism"), which can literally kill us.

Despite monetary success and a perceived winning attitude, statistics from the World Happiness Report 2012 (among other sources) tell us that happiness is not money-based. More importantly, these statistics tell us that most people in today's society are not feeling fulfilled, creatively challenged, or satisfied in their immediate lives. No matter how much success or money you accumulate, it will not buy you inner bliss.

Re-evaluating your life can be a lonely path of emotions, grief, fogginess and indecision. I am here to tell you that you will be okay. It is because you are not alone on this path. Your clarity will improve as you evolve and grow, recognizing that your happiness revolution is based upon gratitude, love, truth, purpose and intuition. The happy backlash is a compassionate movement based on authenticity where all of us on that path can learn to develop a new appreciation for individual uniqueness and collectively thrive.

Failure is not an option when it comes to recognizing and celebrating your uniqueness, as it is the secret sauce to your own billion-dollar brand from the inside out. Remember, the cycles of change are temporary. We have experienced this since 1790 as our ancestors endured and survived more than 200 recessions to date. Most of our ancestors exemplified a survival consciousness with an underlying fear of poverty — what I call "bag lady" mode. This is an extreme practicality adhered to by our grandparents and great-grandparents that may be difficult to understand unless we actually shared the experiences that shaped their views.

Fallen paradigms and worldly structures built upon the survival and integrity of our ancestors represents a death of sorts. It's one in which we must grieve the loss of those before us, whose children and grandchildren have since thrived upon the creations built prior to our birth. We owe a big thank-you to our ancestors who did the best they could on our behalf.

Perhaps the unconscious cloud of grief is where many have become stuck. Grief and loss can take years to overcome, yet we endure, learn from the past, take risks and rebuild, knowing that everything is temporary and `the only direction to go when you are down is UP! It's time to stop hanging low while waiting for a positive life change to come to you.

CHAPTER 2

Riding the Wave of Change

> "If you can change your mind, you can change your life"
> – WILLIAM JAMES

Say YES to LIFE!
Say YES to LOVE!
Say YES to ABUNDANCE!
Say YES to HAPPINESS!
Say YES, PLEASE to YOU!

Your thoughts are directly related to your decisions and acts. Every day you wake up is an anniversary of loving yourself.

Unfortunately, it seems that recognizing this love often is pushed aside as we move day-to-day through our crazy, hectic and stressful world as we run ourselves ragged and into the ground. This is not living life in a courageous or passionate manner. The pervasive feeling of drowning within our own debacle of life and consuming the energy of a collapsing world has us convinced we are collapsing as well.

We have relied on specific chiefs, such as banks, the government, and big corporations, to be the ringleaders of our destinies. Resuscitating our lives, as we once knew it, is not an option. What has become the reliance we must have is upon ourselves. By creating, designing, and manufacturing your own happiness life jacket, you can keep yourself from drowning in the sea of life's daily stresses.

Haphazardly piecing together a life jacket with duct tape and random materials is not exactly the best strategy. It can't give us that a false sense of reassurance that, when we need it for an emergency, it will be an effective floatation device. Instead, the duct-taped life jacket has causes us to become frantic when faced with an impending tsunami. However, we tend to do the best we can with what we have and resort to other strategies like heading to higher ground and taking cover, kissing the sky and thanking God we endured yet another storm safely. In case of an airline disaster, it is always recommended that you put your oxygen mask on first and then you can be of service to others. We can employ the same strategy if we consider leveraging new strategies, tactics, and loving care of self and our fellow man.

To go from performing our best to what is optimal may be a single, more meaningful act of self-love. It's one with significantly more meaning that reincarnates to a heart with know-how! We all have heart, an intention, where we are searching for the "what's in it for me, we, US?" Experiencing paradigm changes and the consequences of change upon us all points to happiness as a healthier choice as we ride the roller coaster surrounded by what is collapsing around us such as economic downturn and instability, corporate greed, and a grandiose sense of entitlement held by many.

When you combine gratitude, meaning, and heart, you revolutionize the act of self -love. Are you doing this for yourself?

Heaviness in your life equates to you putting off what needs a call to action. Examples of this include dealing with debt, marital or relationship issues, or health problems. Passivity ultimately keeps miracles at bay. When you are faithful with what you have, the universe will give you more. You enjoy life more when you get things done with good intentions. Being responsible rewards your good intentions. When you are responsible for your ability to act, to be, to do, inevitably you feel lighter and experience an overall wellness.

Two simple words - "one day"- can cause you to feel unsatisfied, dismayed, and living with regrets for what could have been. What's more, this is a familiarity that leads to a life of complacency that will literally kill you. If you're not busy living and growing, you're simply dying. Many people have come to me who have allowed the past to hold them back. It could be an old experience, regret, sad occurrence or manner in which they had behaved in the past that has led them to a life filled with self-hate or a lack of self-acceptance.

The past contains feelings of yesterday. The only moment that holds your power is the moment right here and now. This is the moment where you can take action to change your life for the better.

"Change Your Destiny" Life Enhancement Exercise

When you're sick and tired of being sick and tired of certain areas of your life, it's now time to clean up the past in your mind and create a new destiny for yourself.

Write out those things from the past that no longer serve you in your life.

> For example, you can start with the statement, *I will no longer:* _____.

Some ideas might be:

> *I will no longer work for no $$$.*
> *I will no longer drink alcohol.*
> *I will no longer tolerate being spoken to with disrespect.*
> *I will no longer eat alone.*

During this exercise, recognize that your feelings are important, but some of your feelings may be a reaction to someone else's standards and not your own feelings of self-worth. Or perhaps your self-worth has diminished because someone has imposed his or her standards on you. Release your resentment, bitterness, or anger related to these people. They are not your friends and are projecting their own pain upon you. Chances are those who choose to judge are unhappy with their own lives.

If this is the case, keep reading. There is more here to help you ride the wave of change as you move toward removing those toxic things that no longer serve you.

Happiness is Not for Sissies, Fear Is!

Happiness is good for your health. Unfortunately, the fact is not all of us are good at predicting what will make us happy or what constitutes well-being. Happiness alone does not lead to a fruitful or fulfilling life. True happiness is an interaction of well-being for the brave who are willing to look at the areas of their lives that can be enhanced or changed for the long-term versus short-term gain.

Your overall well- being encompasses the five elements of well-being. They include:

- Community well-being
- Physical well-being
- Financial well-being
- Career well-being
- Social well-being

According to *Well-Being, the Five Essential Elements*, by Tom Rath and Jim Harter, Ph.D., about 66 percent of the population is thriving in one of the five categories. However, only 7 percent is successfully thriving in all five categories.

As you may already be aware our health is our wealth. The important factors that constitute our well-being include:

- Financial organization and consistency with living within our means
- Relationships of love, intimacy, and social interaction
- A career where you like what you do every day
- And a community life where you like where you live and there is a sense of engagement

To accomplish true happiness and well-being, you must feel deserving of it and recognize the myths and realistic de-stressors.

Don't link your happiness to a small rise in your stock portfolio. **Do** link your happiness to steady time with the people who will lift you up!

Don't wait for a rare opportunity to meet with friends once a year.

Do create more realistic ways in which to spend quality time with friends more often.

Don't buy something to make yourself feel better. **Do** clean out the clutter in your life and donate belongings to help another; you will feel organized and refreshed.

Don't pretend you can do it all with super-hero powers that will burn you out and create resentment. **Do** delegate and accept help from others who care about your health and well-being.

We are living longer, but there are healthier ways in which to do so. Here are some ways that you may not have realized:

Hugs stimulate oxytocin, the "cuddle hormone." There is no such thing as too many friends, so make friends and give hugs!

Strengthen your immune system and decrease stress by meditating. Listen to the *6 Minute a Day Essence Mind* movie that comes with this book. It will improve your mind and stimulate your immune system.

You become more optimistic by writing out what you're thankful for in a gratitude journal.

Get happy and exercise. Thirty minutes a day makes your body's real age 2.8 years younger!

When you change your mood, you can shrink your belly. Cortisol increase and stress play a role when distressed, which adds weight to your mid-section. Change your mood and decrease your belly weight.

Volunteer or support a cause with realistic goals. When you set unrealistic goals, it's a set-up for unhappiness. When you help others and feel a sense of purpose, it's linked to greater happiness.

Yo-yo dieting and quick weight loss scams are unhealthy. Maintain a healthy weight and you will maintain your happiness.

Ten Scientifically-Proven Strategies for Getting Happy

In the last few years, psychologists and researchers have dug deep, finding the hard data to quantify what makes us happy. The emerging field of Positive Psychology has researched and studied people from all over the world to find out how money, attitude, culture, health, memory, altruism and our daily habits affect our well - being. The findings reveal that our actions have a significant effect on our happiness and satisfaction with life. Drum roll, please. The Top 10 proven strategies are:

1. ***Slow down!*** Psychologist Sonya Lyubmorisky studied participants who took time to "savor" ordinary events that are normally hurried through or to think back on pleasant experiences from their day. Her findings showed significant increases in happiness and decreases in depression.

2. ***Focus on your greatest assets and achievements by avoiding comparisons.*** The American culture of keeping up with the Joneses can damage happiness and self-esteem. The more you focus on your personal achievements, the more satisfaction you will experience.

3. ***Don't be a money seeker!*** Did you know the higher you place money on your priority list, the greater your risk for depression, anxiety and low self-esteem. According to Richard Ryan, Professor of Psychology, Psychiatry, and Education at the University of Rochester, "The more we seek material goods, the less we find them there." He says, "The satisfaction has a short half-life — it's very fleeting." Those who sought money also scored lower on tests of self- actualization and vitality.

4. ***Have strong dreams and aspirations!*** This sustains happiness with both pleasure and meaning as the thread for people to have a sense of meaning to thrive. Whether at home or work, the goal is to participate in activities that are both personally enjoyable and pertinent.

5. ***Take initiative.*** Enthusiasm on the work front depends on how much initiative you take. Researcher Amy Wrzesniewski says that, when we express creativity, help others, suggest improvements or do additional tasks, we make our work more rewarding and feel we have more control.

6. ***Find your Happy Tribe.*** Happier people have good friends, families and supportive relationships. Having many acquaintances does not define relationships, but a relationship with understanding and caring does.

7. ***Fake it until you make it.*** The optimist wins over the realist. Intrigued? Optimists think of the future with a glass half-full perspective and make it a habit to have a positive outlook and savor the high points of the past. When you make it a habit to practice a positive outlook, even if you were born with a glass half-empty perspective, you can make positivity a habit if you practice it.

8. ***Get Writing.*** Write your gratitude list and goals. Research has revealed that, if you keep a journal and write on a weekly basis, you score higher on the happiness scale and lower on the depression scale and remain this way for many weeks. Those who achieved this are more likely to make progress on their personal goals and tend to be healthier and more optimistic.

9. ***Get Moving.*** A Duke University study showed that exercise may be more effective than drugs in treating depression. Exercise not only boosts endorphins, but the feel-good hormone also improves one's sense of accomplishment.

10. ***When you give, you gain.*** Helping a neighbor, volunteering, celebrating a friend's accomplishment or spending money on others as opposed to one's self results in a "helpers high" The helper's high actually allows you to gain more health benefits than you would from exercising or stopping tobacco use.

Fifty scientific studies funded through The Institute for Research on Unlimited Love, headed by Stephen G. Post, Ph.D., a professor of Bioethics at the Case Western University School of Medicine, found overall, helpers high reduces stress for the benevolent individual and the recipient. Two large studies found that older adults who volunteered reaped health and dwell-being benefits. Those who volunteered were living longer than non-volunteers. Post reports that another large study found a 44 percent reduction in early deaths among those who consistently and frequently volunteered — a greater effect than exercising four times a week.

Research has shown HAPPINESS:

Decreases stress

Encourage weight loss

Decreases heart disease

Makes you look young

Boosts relationships

It's FREE

Brain chemicals also play an important role in altruistic behavior. Studies have identified high levels of the "bonding" hormone oxytocin in people who are very generous towards others. Oxytocin is a hormone best known for its role in preparing mothers for motherhood. Studies have also shown that this hormone helps both men and women establish trusting relationships. In fact, oxytocin may be associated with physical and emotional well-being. According to Gregory Fricchione, M.D., Associate Professor of Psychiatry at Harvard Medical School, "Oxytocin is the mediator of what has been called the 'tend-mend' response to stress. When you're altruistic and touching people in a positive way, lending a helping hand, your oxytocin level goes up, and that relieves your own stress." Studies looked at numerous effects that oxytocin can produce in lab rates — lower blood pressure, lower levels of stress hormone and an overall calming effect.

CHAPTER 3

If Money Does Not Buy Happiness, What Does?

"Money never made a man happy yet, nor will it. The more a man has the more he wants. Instead of filling a vacuum, it makes one."
– BENJAMIN FRANKLIN

If there was ever a time to learn our karmic lessons as a nation regarding economic happiness, it is now! The United States, land of the free and home of the smiley face, has paid dearly for our freedom, and our credit score is a reflection of a free-spending society. Competition over excess has led to greed, fear and an increase in fraud. No doubt, our level of happiness on a conscious level has been linked to money. In fact, money has imprinted the reflection of our nation's spending upon us on many levels, especially the illusion of well-being. The question remains: Who are we really when stripped of our money?

Like anything, money is energy much like a wave, continuously flowing in and out, toward us and away from us. How it flows and is measured has become the question at hand. It is clear that Gross Domestic Product (GDP) is no longer a satisfactory or credible form of measuring our economic health and prosperity. The groundswell occurred after

Nobel Prize-winning economist Joseph Stiglitz surmised in a 2009 report, entitled "Report of the Commission on the Measurement of Economic Performance and Social Progress", following the 2008 global economic crisis, stated, "The time is ripe ... to shift emphasis from measuring economic production to measuring people's well-being."

Several cities and states are exploring citizen well-being or "floating happiness initiatives." The pursuit of this measure is to build momentum on a worldwide level for environmental and social welfare reasons as well. As I write this book, a federally-funded panel is studying whether there is a better way to tally prosperity. This issue harkens back to the 1960s when Robert F. Kennedy spoke in March 1968 about "the gross national product as measuring everything in short, except that which makes life worthwhile, the beauty of our poetry, health of our children, quality of their education or the strength of our marriages."

Money may be tied to happiness to a degree; however, money is just one of many factors related to joy, fulfillment and what is best for the greater good. Studies show that happiness scores do not increase for individuals who earn an average of $75,000 per year. Although it is difficult to measure subjective feelings, such as gratitude, it remains relevant that we practice gratitude as a form of increasing happiness in our lives.

There is much speculation surrounding the metrics of well-being and happiness in relation to the age-old question about whether money buys happiness. The more we recognize that we are each responsible for our own happiness, the closer we are to seeing that our happiness powers the way to improved relationships, career, finances, health, and quality of life issues.

Earlier, I defined conscious happiness as the ability to deliberately change an old perspective with a new, positive action. As a world, if we embrace the happiness revolution, it will be a time of awakening where the tsunami of consciousness will be a welcome change, where the old world paradigms will be released and new world paradigms will be created. This is beyond measurement and become more of a humanitarian effort where economists are beginning to take heed.

Do we have the power to create a good and happy life now without sacrificing lives in the future? In other words, we may have become wealthier over time, but we also have become sicker. The "work hard, play hard" mentality has affected the head, heart and health of each one of us. It has become so critical that, as a nation, the quality of our well-being, life expectancy, and ecological footprint scored 36.1 on a scale of zero to 100 in the 2012 Happiness Planet Index (HPI) The HPI index measures these components to the extent to which countries have citizens with long, happy, and sustainable lives. Of the 151 countries measured, the HPI ranks countries on how many long and happy lives they produce per unit of environmental input.

Naturally, there is room for improvement and perhaps we can learn from the countries that, rich or poor, have been successful based on areas of concentration which the United States has overlooked. If we were to look at what we can measure differently, beyond economics, perhaps the measurement of production and consumption will be efficient.

Where we are investing our efforts for a sustainable and happy country has been talked about by the U.S. government, yet we continue to hold on to what we have out of fear, greed, and a negative lineage of our egos that tricks us into listening more to the negative with limited action to connect to the positive. As spiritual teacher and author Eckhart Tolle surmised, "The primary cause of unhappiness is never the situation but thought about it. Be aware of the thoughts you are thinking. Separate them from the situation, it is as it is. Humanity is now faced with a stark choice: evolve or die. If the structures of the human mind remain unchanged, we will always end up re-creating the same world, the same evils, and the same dysfunction."

Perhaps the "economics of happiness" may be a solution that can work as it has in the happiest of places surveyed in the HPI: Costa Rica, Denmark and Bhutan.

What has Costa Rica accomplished that we can learn from? Positive action, such as investment in education and health versus armed forces, has been shown to be a much better investment for increasing a more stable society while boosting the economy and improving quality of life as surveyed in HPI 2012.

Denmark, known to be a wealthy society and one of the planet's happiest countries in 2007, links happiness to the public perception of safety and an emphasis on investment in social equality and robust welfare policies.

Ideally, what would the land of Happiness Economics look like?

Imagine a land of clean air, natural beauty, smiling happy faces and a sustainable existence where all felt good in the world and stress barely existed among the population. Divorce rate is low, the number of tourists is high, and everyone benefits financially based upon a "flow" of monies initiated by the king of the land. This is a country where no one went hungry or homeless. Is this utopian existence real and, if so, how can we learn from it? Not only is it real, but it also has been portrayed as the link to happiness despite remaining as a poor country.

The land of happiness economics is Bhutan, a small country in Southeast Asia between China and India whose primary focus is Gross National Happiness rather than Gross National Product. Although more than 30 percent of Bhutan's people are in material poverty, GDP per capita is among the highest in South Asia and it has made tremendous strides in education and tackling malaria. The country recognizes a need to modernize, but it is attempting to do so within the framework of its Buddhist values. It acknowledges the importance of economic growth, but it also encourages the promotion of culture and heritage as well as the preservation and sustainable use of the environment.

Gross National Happiness comprises nine components of happiness in Bhutan and can be quantifiably measured:

- Psychological well-being
- Ecology
- Health
- Education
- Culture
- Living standards
- Time use
- Community vitality
- Good governance

In essence, Bhutan focuses on the pursuit of happiness and well-being in the face of public and policy debate as opposed to the acquisition of consumption, materialism and production.

In Buddhism, happiness is determined by the qualities of being. This means being fully human and alive with sharing compassion, cooperation, shared knowledge and imagination as components to achieving happiness. Inherent in Buddhism is the idealistic and unorthodox approach to measuring progress that questions the values of capitalism and neoclassical economics as they relate to balance, harmony and altruism.

Does this mean we all should decide to turn to Buddhism? Not necessarily, but what it does imply the viability of a universal mindset that revolves around kindness to self and toward others, respect for nature, and the attraction of abundance beyond materialism.

Skeptical? According to British economist and founder of the Centre for Economic Performance, Sir Richard Layard, "There is a common fear that governments trying to promote happiness will become over-bossy — the Nanny State. The fear is misplaced. From a mass of evidence, we know the huge importance of freedom as a cause of happiness. The most miserable countries ever recorded were those in the Soviet bloc. No one who used evidence to promote happiness would go down that route."

There are many forms of freedom. In many places in the world, there is freedom from arbitrary arrest, freedom to speak your mind, and so on. But, there is also freedom to choose your job and your lifestyle. It was for this reason that Adam Smith preached the importance of the free market while at the same time he urged governments to promote happiness. The two are not mutually exclusive. Smith noted, "Since we live in society, we are deeply affected by how other people behave. As we become richer, this issue assumes ever-greater importance. So we now see governments reorienting their interest in the direction of behavior. This is good. We do not want a society of conformists, but we do want a society where people really care about each other's happiness."

As Thomas Jefferson, hardly a conformist, said: "The care of human life and happiness and not their destruction is the only legitimate object of good government. And, to do the job, governments will have to measure happiness."

Being happy and choosing happiness is not for sissies. If you want to be happy, you have to show it, exude it. Happiness is beyond being a choice; it is an action. After all, happiness is contagious! A recent study has shown that, when you spend monies on others as opposed to yourself, you feel good! When you feel good, you behave in a manner where you repeat behaviors. Your actions encourage others to feel good and you feel good expressing happy actions.

Where Does the U.S. Rank with Life Satisfaction, Well-Being, and Economics?

Building a theory about and measurement of "happynomics" is not an easy one. If it were, what would the results actually do for us?

Each year, the Organization for Economic Cooperation and Development produces the Better Life Index, a comprehensive report on the well-being of advanced countries. Well-being and the "good life" are subjective. There is no right or wrong when it comes to personal happiness or the value behind one's well-being. In other words, some people prefer living in a small home versus a larger one. Others are geared toward making money where some are not as concerned about money as they are about quality of time.

The Better Life Index is comprised of 11 components that have been identified as being essential to material living and quality of life. These include:

- income
- jobs
- Housing
- Community
- Education
- Environment
- Health
- Life Satisfaction
- Civic Engagement
- Safety
- Work-life Balance

In comparison to 39 countries that participated in the index, how does the United States stack up and what do the results tell us as a society?

Overall, Americans are the wealthiest, but not necessarily the happiest. But while the U.S. ranked number one in making more money than other happier countries, Americans work long hours, take fewer vacations and spend less time socializing with friends and family. The United States also has the largest gaps between the rich and poor with the top 20 percent of the population earning nearly $82,000 a year while the bottom 20 percent earned just $10,600 annually.

What is wrong with this picture?

Americans live in a nation of the haves and have-nots, where the middle class is heading toward invisibility, where the country of plenty has more than 15 million starving children, and where 62 percent of teachers witness children coming to school hungry. If the country continues in the same direction, these numbers will certainly increase.

Much of the happiness in American society has been relative to external factors as opposed to internal feelings. Professor Richard Easterlin, Professor of Economics at the University of Southern California, noted the paradox of the United States where, at any particular time, richer individuals are happier than poorer ones, yet, over time, society did not become happier as it became richer. Not surprisingly, individuals who tended to compare themselves to others were happier when on the higher social or income ladder. However, when everybody rises together, relative status remains unchanged. While higher income may raise happiness to an extent, it also can reduce happiness. Repeatedly, psychologists have found that individuals who put a high premium on higher incomes are generally less happy and more vulnerable to psychological issues than individuals who do not crave higher incomes.

According to the 2012 World Happiness Report, "Affluence has created its own set of afflictions and addictions, such as obesity, adult-onset diabetes, and tobacco-related illnesses, eating disorders such as anorexia and bulimia, and psychosocial disorders. Addictions to shopping, TV and gambling are all examples of disorders of development. So, too, is the loss of community, the decline of social trust, and the rising anxiety levels associated with the vagaries of the modern globalized economy, including the threats of unemployment or episodes of illness not covered by health insurance in the United States."

There is a principle that shows that poor people benefit far more from an added dollar of income than rich people. Overwhelming research shows that gains in well-being are very small to those who expect to become happier by becoming richer. Life satisfaction (or happiness) is easily improved upon based on the proportion of household income otherwise known as the "diminishing marginal utility of income." For example, a poor household at $1,000 income requires an extra $100 to raise its life satisfaction as opposed to a rich household at a $1,000,000 income, which would need 1,000 times more money, or $100,000, to raise its well-being by the same notch.

Economists base their theories on the fact that individuals are rational decision makers who know what they want and are able to remain within their given budget. The rationale of a Gross National Product is largely based upon excess of consumption in association to improvement in life conditions of the poor. The perceived proportionate measure based on a disproportionate society is a comparison of apples to oranges. For example, increased consumption of gasoline and oil is based on price, and reflects a healthy economy based on the GDP. However, in this case, the increase is based on cost, but does not equate to value to the consumer.

The advertising industry, a $500 billion behemoth, beats the drum for creating demand, selling products, and equating "things" with happiness. It has turned even our youngest children into savvy consumers (what two-year old doesn't equate going to the local fast food restaurant with receiving a children's meal in a box containing a toy?).Americans spend billions of dollars on any variety of advertised products while advertisers prey upon psychological weakness and entice with products associated with high social status rather than real needs.

American Spending in 2012

This can be seen in the data collected on what Americans spent in 2012 (partial year) on various product and service categories:

Have the personal values of families and individuals been lost among the distraction of excess? The behavior of indulgence and collection of excess appears as a false illusion of happiness among Americans, which unconsciously serves as a form of intimacy distancing. It simultaneously is forming a rift in community and individuals' personal truth. This is what I term as "living by the Nile." The layers of denial seem to grow to a point where you don't realize how deep you are in until you can no longer paddle upstream. You essentially become extremely exhausted by the efforts of paddling in the wrong direction; this leaves many people feeling out of control, overwhelmed, frustrated, isolated, and unhappy.

The 2012 World Happiness Report noted: "GNP is a valuable goal, but should not be pursued to the point where economic stability is jeopardized, community cohesion is destroyed, the vulnerable are not supported, ethical standards are sacrificed, or the world's climate is put at risk. While basic living standards are essential for happiness, after the baseline has been met happiness varies more with quality of human relationships than income. Other policy goals should include high employment and high-quality work; a strong community with high levels of trust and respect, which government can influence through inclusive participatory policies; improved physical and mental health; support of family life; and a decent education for all. Four steps to improve policy-making are the measurement of happiness, explanation of happiness, putting happiness at the center of analysis, and translation of well-being

Americans spending in 2012

FOOD & BEVERAGES
Groceries: $478 Billion
Fast Food: $117 Billion
Beer: $96 Billion
Soda: $65 Billion
Chocolate: $16 Billion
Coffee: $11 Billion

Child Care: $47 Billion
Gambling: $ 34.6 Billion

MEDICINE
Alternative Medicine: $33.9 Billion
Prescription Drugs: $320 Billion

Professional Sports: $25.4 Billion
Tattoos: $2.3 Billion
Tattoo Removal: $66 Million

TECHNOLOGY: $ 1.2 Trillion
Electronic devices, computers/PC's, mobile services,
online gambling, texting, video services, TV/Cable

Video Games: $17 Billion
Weight Loss: $60 Billion

American Gaming Assoc., Brewers Assoc., Consumer Report, Fast Food Mktg., Franchise Direct, Gartner,
IBIS, IMS, INC, Market data, National Soft Drink Assoc., NPD, USDA, WR Hambrecht)

research into design and delivery of services." The latter remains to be seen in the United States. However, Bhutan has set a new precedent. There, Gross National Happiness has blazed a new trail and the pillars of government policy far exceed Gross National Product.

Defining and Achieving Your Happiness

How one defines and measures the quality of life satisfaction, personal well-being and overall happiness has been difficult; most experts in this area have not agreed because of economic fluctuations, changes in carbon footprints, and vast cultural and societal differences. Separate from looking to policymakers as defining a U.S. happiness index, perhaps it is more important to form a stronger link with re-establishing individual happiness related to personal life satisfaction, household and well-being.

Ask anyone on the street what they most want and the majority will tell you happiness. If you were to ask the 14th Dalai Lama, Tenzin Gyatso, what is the purpose of life, he would tell you, "I believe the purpose of life is to be happy." To achieve happiness, the Dali Lama simply believes we should devote our most serious efforts to bringing about mental peace. The more we care about the happiness of others, the greater our own sense of well-being becomes. This sentiment would entail a selfless mindset. Often, this is where love and compassion grows and hinders anger and hate. By detoxing the inner pain, you can build an inner strength.

If you prefer a simple formula for happiness, Mahatma Gandhi believed anyone who is not focused on self has no fears. His equation for happiness looks like this:

$$[R]esources/Pertinent\ [N]eed = [H]appiness$$

On-command resources when needed equal happiness — the fewer the needs, the greater the increase of happiness. Think about it: When your basic needs are met, are you usually in a happy state? You are rested, have food in your stomach, monies to cover your supplies, and a place where you can bathe, eat, and sleep. Simple, right?

Yet, how do we manage our desires? Dr. Madan Kataria, originator of Laughter Yoga, shared an interesting viewpoint, "We all have desires and there is no way we can escape, but personally I found the answer. If your desires are directed to the self, they are bound to make you miserable, but if they are directed to help others, they will enrich your life, and you can have as many as you want. The second most important thing about desires is — don't get attached to the outcome. If they get fulfilled it is good, if not it is still very good! There is a right time for everything in life. Everything happens for a reason. Just go with the flow."

How do we differentiate between being lacking, having enough, and abundance? In the U.S., we often have fairly concrete expectations in our minds that define how much money we can accumulate, what our soul mate should look like, what our job should entail, and how others should behave based upon their titles. When reality does not meet up with our expectations, we are disappointed. Yet, there are other areas of our lives in which we are abundant, but we don't pay attention for whatever reason.

In fact, we are all naturally abundant in all areas of our lives. Once you change your understanding and belief of the unmet area of abundance, you open up a new channel for abundance to come in to your life. For example, have you ever noticed that there are people who easily make money in their lives, where others have struggled in this area of abundance? Perhaps you were taught that money is the root of all evil. This is a belief that may be blocking this area of abundance for you as you are resisting what you believe is evil on an unconscious level. When you redefine your belief of money the possibilities of attracting it becomes greater. When we let go of a defined expectation and are not looking, abundance comes in a much more fulfilling way and in a package that was not what was envisioned.

Our society may hold a similar box thinking surrounding the well-being and happynomics of the United States, where we have an old definition of abundance and feel the economic cliff should be resolved in a specific manner, with an expectation that policy holders and government key holders have the answers. Instead, we can embrace change, be the architects of our reality, and release old crutches, which have little to do with Gross Domestic Product and more to do with Gross Domestic Happiness. We are the ones who are capable of developing and empowering a new measure.

The secret behind the power of Gross Domestic Happiness has more to do with imagination and innovation and less to do with fixing what has been broken for a long time. This does not imply we leave behind people as the consequence of what is broken but rather push new life towards possibility as we all realign with the goal of renewal in mind. Realistically, facing our fears head on and releasing waste in our lives is a crucial first step in the acknowledgement that happiness has its up and downs, as part of the growth process.

How do we know and understand what happiness is without sadness or fear being part of the equation? I believe if we are to live in our truth and operate out of integrity much like Gandhi states about happiness: "(Happiness) is when what you think, what you say and what you do are in harmony." To fully embrace feeling ALIVE, you can empower yourself through your thoughts, feelings, and actions. This is part of creating a new-found freedom.

Gross Domestic Happiness

The determination to improve your life satisfaction, well-being, and happiness entails asking yourself questions that you may find fleeting, yet are important in improving the quality of your life, the quality of what you buy, and the quality of our growing nation's society in both health and wealth. For example, the desire of the moment has a vast difference than the true desire that serves your authentic self. Your authentic self is the core of who you are, the qualities that make you unique, the inner genius of who you are meant to be, not who you believe you are supposed to represent based on a role or function in life. All the things compose your wisdom that needs genuine and true expression.

Fulfilling our desire of the moment — watch an hour of TV instead of taking a walk or surfing the Internet instead of getting our work done — are distractions that are simply a temporary stress reliever.

Fulfilling your authentic self — making an extra effort to get your work done so you have quality time with those you love or exercising your body so you feel good, healthy and vital — is the way to grow and share, to be and do all you can. This is what encourages lasting fulfillment, joy and happiness.

The decisions we make may be based on new or different internal questions where your job and motivation are to maximize your own happiness, kindness, and health for the overall greater good. And perhaps make better choices in the moment.

Internal questions include: Would you rather have a new TV or a new friendly neighbor? Would you rather job security or a pay raise? Would you rather have a bigger house or more free time?

How we create harmony in our life is EMPOWERING! Once we follow our truth, we have the power to change the world toward the positive.

As far back as 1968, a few months prior to his death, Bobby Kennedy proclaimed the narrow viewpoint in which we base the progress of our lives, our organizations and our communities with shallow measures. Kennedy surmised a point that has caught up to us currently when he described, our lives are the composite of much more than our economic output. Of which:

"We seem to have surrendered community excellence and community values in the mere accumulation of material things. Our gross domestic product... if we should judge America by that — counts air pollution and cigarette advertising and ambulances to clear our highways of carnage. It counts special locks for our doors and jails for the people who break them down. It counts the destruction of our redwoods and the loss of our natural wonder in chaotic sprawl. It counts napalm and the cost of a nuclear warhead, and armored cars for police who fight riots in our streets. It counts (Charles) Whitman's rifle and (Richard) Speck's knife, and the television programs that glorify violence in order to sell toys to our children. Yet, the gross domestic product does not allow for the health of our children, the quality of their education, or the joy of their play. It does not include the beauty of our poetry or the strength of our marriages; the intelligence of our public debate or the integrity of our public officials. It measures neither wit nor courage; neither our wisdom nor our learning; neither our compassion nor our devotion to our country; it measures everything, in short, except that which makes life worthwhile."

To encourage what is worthwhile calls for a new measurement that surveys the capacity of what actually is worthwhile and directly measures the happiness and well–being of our nation in relation to those worthwhile factors (this concept also applies to individuals). Hence, by adapting a new measurement of Gross Domestic Happiness, we could create a shift in recognizing what we value the most, and investing in those values, to be in place for the long term. The resurrection and preservation of the greater good in our communities, organizations and lives has a stronger chance through a new mindset and change in what we feel is really important to us as people, members of families, and citizens. Our economic health now relies on Gross Domestic Happiness, more so than ever, to improve the happiness of business and life.

Real Happiness

First, you need to ask: Are you taking actions in your life out of fear or love?

What gets you closer to your divine purpose and mission is best based on love and feeling centered within yourself — to feel your feelings

Gross Domestic Happiness® **Transcends** GROSS DOMESTIC PRODUCT.

- Jackie Ruka

and act in an authentic manner based upon what feels right to you, not what you feel others want or expect.

When you access and practice your passions every day, you are serving your happiness. This is more of what sets the basis for real happiness.

Appointing yourself as your own happyologist is a great starting point in which to zone in on self and qualify your well-being, your joy, and your level of fulfillment. Like a three-legged stool, are the three legs balanced and sustained? As we grow, the legs of happiness may need adjustment and lead you to reassess your well-being, life satisfaction and level of happiness.

Ask yourself this one question to help define your authentic purpose and level of happiness: imagine if money was not a concern. What would you be doing with your life?

" It always seems impossible until it's done."
– NELSON MANDELA

Detoxify
Your
Life

CHAPTER 4

The Secret to Hitting the Rest Button

The Art of Deliberate Creation

Einstein once said, "I am enough of an artist to draw freely upon my imagination. Imagination is more important than knowledge. Knowledge is limited. Imagination encircles the world." He was a master of deliberate creation. Using the Universal Law of **Deliberate Creation** you deliberately create your reality instead of letting your life happen to you by default. When your life seems to be out of control and you don't have the things that you want, it is only because you created it that way. You didn't do it on purpose, but you did create every part of your life."

Did you know that there is a powerful process that has been practiced by great historians, engineers, artists and presidents over the centuries, including recognized geniuses such as Michelangelo, Thomas Edison, Ben Franklin, John F. Kennedy, Pablo Picasso, John Lennon, Mark Twain, Steve Jobs, Bill Gates, Steven Spielberg and Walt Disney? This process has manifested theories, global shifts, economic changes and peace treaties as well as many of the creative tools and brilliant inventions that we use routinely every day - ranging from electricity to the iPad. What is it? It is exercising the whole brain at once by systematically balancing the use of both the right and left hemispheres.

The brain is the sexiest and most fascinating of the human organs. Your entire makeup, ranging from your personality and behavior, five senses, sense of humor, thinking, perception and reasoning operate out of the soul, which is the headquarters of our nervous system. Your brain took charge of your human functions on every level of your existence as you entered this world. You are a miracle!

Of course, the brain is still by far an organ that also holds mystery. Why we say what we say, do what we do, act as we do and feel as perplexed or confused as we do seem to have no precision to it. Yet, the brain creates all those things for you while it is the same organ that defines your logic and dictates moments for digging deep.

The term, "thinking out of the box," in most cases means asking your right brain to go beyond what is familiar to it. The brain's left hemisphere usually breaks things down as well as quantifies and conjures up data for determining results. When you add right brain activities to the mix, you can use creativity and imagination to think beyond limits by looking at the whole picture rather than snippets of them. While you can practice the use of the whole brain, one hemisphere may be dominant for you.

A fun aspect of the process I teach is watching the complementary mind movie that comes with the book. Whether you are left-brain dominant or right-brain dominant, you'll find that the mind movie relaxes your left hemisphere and enhances the function of the right brain at the same time. The benefit of watching the mind movie on a regular basis is you more consistently think outside of your box and your imagination is invigorated. Exercising the "muscle" of your imagination sets the basis for your subconscious to deliver powerful new ideas and "aha" moments to you in your conscious reality.

Remember, the imagination (your mind's eye) serves as the key that unlocks the door to your inner treasures, setting the stage for self-discovery. By calling upon your powers of imagination, your ability to conceptualize, create, and manifest your desires becomes clearer, thus setting the tone for the deliberate creation process.

How to Get Started on a New Journey

The process that you will learn below is my interpretation of the Universal Law of Deliberate Creation, which I formed through my own journey of self-discovery as well as by conducting more than 5,000 hours of therapy sessions with different clients. The secrets I learned combine knowledge gleaned from my experience as an artist, psychotherapist, healer and corporate professional.

Now, these have morphed into a pragmatic process for developing happiness and expressing our desires and talents while respecting fate.

This can be somewhat of a dance that includes knowing when to stop, wait, turn and move forward in an intuitive direction with the universe. In most cases, you will find the universe is whispering in your ear to bring forth a gift or burning desire. It is up to you to listen carefully and attune yourself to the calling so that you can answer back to the universe. This is known as your intuition; always follow it.

While you are traveling your new path, you may occasionally stumble or encounter some apprehension/fear or a block that is interfering in your progress. The mind mantras and intentional exercises in this guidebook are your tools for navigating away from the shadows and negativity. The clearer you become, the easier it will be to move toward your heart's true desire.

A Call to Action

I fine-tuned this particular process when I was responding to my calling from the universe and discovered I needed to sell my home. Amazingly, not only did I sell my home at the height of the 2008 recession, but I also sold it in one week for my asking price (the number I imagined) to a buyer that I termed in my mind as the perfect "cash" buyer. By imagining this outcome and imagining myself co-creating it with the "right" like-minded real estate agent for my neighborhood, I knew there was the potential for an easy and smooth response to my offer that would lead to the house being sold.

The timing of selling my home could not have been worse. There was a short-sale home across the street that had been sitting on the market for almost a year. Down the street, several other larger homes, whose prices were lower than mine, were up for sale. By comparison, my home appeared overpriced; however, this was a perspective on the situation that I would not allow to defeat me.

As I began deliberately co-creating this reality, an important feeling took hold of me: I had an absolutely positive belief that the house was already sold and no longer mine. This motivated me to start cleansing the energy of the house. I smudged its every corner with sage while repeating the mantra, "I release this house to its greater good." In addition to the spiritual cleansing I had done, I physically cleansed it, throwing out every piece of junk in the house that I had been hanging onto for no meaningful reason. I also sold valuable items I possessed that no longer served a purpose for me but could be useful for others.

The most important component in the process that had to take place if this home sale was to occur was to step into the place within myself that I wanted to be and to feel with all of my being what it would be like to let go of the part of my life that was ending so a new part of my life could begin. I prepared myself with a major emotional release and by depersonalizing that which was no longer mine. In this way, I knew that the ideal buyer could feel the house as his or her own upon entering the structure. I also arranged the house so it would feel like a relaxing vacation home, including a few nice and unexpected surprises here and there. When visitors left, I intended for them to feel a relaxing resonance, hopefully prompting an alignment with the perfect buyer among them.

Luck and timing may play an important role in some areas of our lives, but when we are ready to set radical change into motion, we can do so more effectively by controlling as many aspects of our surroundings as we can. Through acts of deliberate creation, you can remove any sense of inner desperation or perceived obstacles. In turn, your light shines very brightly for all to see and attracts that with which you specifically align.

Many synchronistic events occurred following the sale of my home, and I am happy to report that the universe and I are happily in sync.

The Seven Essential Ingredients to Get Happy and Create a Kick-Butt Life

Do you yearn to set your heart's true desire in motion? Your starting point is the answer to the one question you must ask and listen to: What is your heart's true desire?

Write your heart's true desire here:_____.

When you're feeling ready, follow the steps of deliberate creation and enjoy the power of the process in which you are immersed. There are no weird coincidences. What is meant to be always happens — and you have the power to deliberately create an ideal outcome. Your success is indicated by the power of your will to overcome obstacles with the narrowing down of the areas of interest. Based on focused intention, we often lose focus on less important areas so as to focus intently on the one.

The seven steps of deliberate creation are:

1. imagining
2. forming your vision
3. experiencing stages of Universal Change
4. trusting the Universe
5. Actively co-creating
6. Shifting
7. Linking

Let's take a look at each one of these steps more closely.

1. ***Imagining.*** Imagine that you are a blank canvas, the tabula rasa of a new life, or a new next chapter, turning a corner in any direction you care to take. For you to proceed with momentum and clarity, you must tap into your feelings and shed your ego. Sounds like an oxymoron. How can you shed your ego and tap into your feelings without using those wonderful defense mechanisms to protect you from the fear of rejection, fear of success, or fear of scrutiny by others? Simple. It only takes six minutes a day of dedicated time for just you, in which you will slowly, gently enter a new universe where your subconscious mind rests.

   By slowly tapping into your light, the colors within the rainbow of who you can free you from the material things that you are hanging onto for no apparent reason. In so doing, the guided imagery you use sets the tone for a whole new you to be born in each and every new day. Uncovering and discovering begins to take place and opens your heart to receive positivity. Remember, the opposite of fear is love. Opening your mind opens your heart. Guided imagery is a safe method for this process. Studies now show that six to 12 minutes a day of silencing your mind increases blood flow to the brain and sharpens your judgment and decision-making abilities.

   Watch and listen to the mind movie at the start or end of your day or if you have not yet been introduced to visual meditation, please visit **www.gethappyguide.com**.

2. ***Forming your vision.*** We each can access a left-brain hemisphere and a right-brain hemisphere mode of thinking. Logic, numbers and analytical thinking lie within the left side of the brain. Imagination, creativity, visualization and perspective reside within the right side of the brain. Some people are right dominant; others are left dominant. No matter which one you are, you can benefit by opening up the right-brain hemisphere. This is where you will learn tap into your true desires. In the left side of the brain, there is a different process that is essential to deliberate creation, which I call linking. Linking is where your left hemisphere associates your passions with and relays them to the external world. More on linking is discussed later in the book.

3. *Going through stages of universal change.* Psychologist Irvin Yalom identified these stages. In his book, "Group Dynamics," he explains that whenever a group of new people is brought together for a specific purpose, the roles of the participants become defined as the group evolves. Perhaps you have led or participated in a church or support group or joined a company where you have seen this happening. Yalom's "forming, storming, norming and performing" circle defines the dynamics that occur as the group progresses.

    As your personal happiness movement gets under way, the stages you go through may resemble the stages of group dynamics. Determining which stage you are in can serve as a barometer to measure your progress in communing with the universe. This can help you form a bird's eye view of where you are in the big picture of the journey. Of course, each path is different as will the amount of time that is spent in each stage. Your Plan A may change into your Plan B that, in turn, may propel you closer to performing as needed to reach your personal goals, realistically and effectively.

4. *Trusting the universe.* Deliberate creation requires possessing a strong belief in yourself and the universe, which protects you by helping you make the right decisions or alerting you to go in a different direction. Your intuition plays a role in the trust process. If you ignore intuition, you won't feel good about what you are getting into. But, if you set aside stubbornness and ego and enter into a state of "allowance," all you have to do is to wait and listen. Soon, you will receive a sign. This sign prompts a feeling of "yes" or "uh oh." So, stay clear and allow. Remember, a state of allowance may manifest something that does not look like what you thought it would. If this happens, pay attention to how you feel. Check in and examine your feelings. Hanging onto your initial perspective may bring on a wall of resistance, yet you can trust the universe has put what you want in front of you.

    For example, my client, Janet, was ready for a relationship. She knew that she detested being with a man who was a sports fanatic and did not appreciate her cooking. Her family history included a father who was a compulsive gambler and did not show his kids much attention or love. Janet served as the parent-child of the family, cooking and taking care of her younger siblings while her parents ran the family restaurant. Janet was an excellent cook and spent many hours making sumptuous meals; this was her way of showing nurturance and love. But, her siblings did not appreciate her for her cooking, and her parents rarely rewarded her for all of her efforts.

Upon meeting Dan, a tall, gregarious, self-determined man, Janet felt excited. However, Dan was an avid golfer and held season tickets for all the professional baseball and football games in town. If he was not at a game, he was watching every game on the weekends. Dan grew up in a household where no one cooked and he was content eating TV dinners. His palate for cuisine was unsophisticated. As she discovered these things about Dan, Janet's initial excitement soon turned to doubt and apprehension. Yet, when she spent time with Dan, he gave her his undivided attention and was willing to put aside his sports game schedule to get to know her. This made her feel wanted and adored.

Dan soon embraced Janet's cooking and he felt good about her taking care of him. It was a winning combination. Despite her initial resistance, Janet was able to co-create a happy existence with Dan that matched her heart's true desire of creating a loving, committed marriage with a willing partner thanks to her feeling of allowance, listening, and trusting the universe.

5. *Actively co-creating.* Deliberate manifestation requires expressing your desires and intention through networking with others. This requires "due diligence" that includes researching and acting to support your intention in a way that goes beyond just goal setting. It also involves affirming the intention so it is heard and taken seriously is a must. This sets the synchronistic wheels of the universe in motion for you. The universe moves your intention into reality by matching it to the outer world, chewing on it, and spitting back a timely response.

For example, you're headed to the bookstore with a particular subject in mind, such as resume writing. You walk into the bookstore and head straight to the career section. However, the heading of a book that captures your attention in the New Age section sidetracks you. You pick up the book and start reading, and next thing you know, you are intrigued and excited about what this book is sharing with you — so much so, in fact, that you buy the New Age book and your motivation to find a book on writing a resume is lost. The answer for what you truly were seeking was placed directly in front of you and you felt compelled to reach out to it. It was not an error. This is an example of the universe answering you back in a way that may set you on a path of your heart's true desire. So, pay attention to the clues you get while acting upon an intention.

6. *Shifting.* During deliberate creation, the universe may cause a shift in you in response to it, or you may proactively create a shift to which the universe responds. Any event that deeply affects you is an opportunity for a shift as it presents you with a glimpse of your mortality and what is truly important to you. A shift repositions your perspective on your role and purpose in an area of your life. With every ending, there is a beginning. As you travel toward your new path, the mantras and tools presented in this book can be used for reference and to help you transition smoothly during your reinvention so as to crystallize a new path and what you have to offer. As this becomes clear, you will be prepared to position yourself to proactively and deliberately create a shift to which the universe will positively respond.

7. *Linking (or re-purposing).* During the reinvention process, you will access your strengths and build on them to see where they fit in the world. All the mini-accomplishments you make during this process will help you to expand your options. As you open your world to new possibilities, you also link yourself to the people and systems that can bring forth abundance from these possibilities. Purposefully forming new links is a left-brain-oriented activity. When you set a new path into motion, new links will manifest. This happens even as you are simultaneously cultivating your craft and elevating your life to a level that is entirely new and different from your past. It is how your personal vision is being fed by your actions.

Three Levels of Happiness, Which One Are You?

"You cannot travel the path, until you become the path itself."
– BUDDHA

We are all responsible for our own happiness — this is nothing new. However, have you ever wondered if this is as good as it gets?

Perhaps your definition of happiness has changed over the years as you have. It may be time to re-evaluate what your happiness set point is and determine a new path.

Did you know that your happiness could exponentially grow? According to the Vedas, the oldest scriptures of Hinduism, happiness is a subjective topic. For example, a person, place or thing at one time represented happiness to you and another time brought misery. Knowing you are responsible for your own happiness or sorrow helps with realizing that you are not responsible for external stimuli of the world.

> ***Stage 1: Basic or worldly happiness.*** Worldly happiness is enjoyment to a certain extent. This could include singing, dancing, drinking, material items, money, a perfect body, life without disease, etc. Yet, these involve external stimuli, which is temporary as is the effect it may have on your happiness.

> ***Stage 2: Temporary joy or flow of happiness.*** As an artist and writer, I term my mental happiness as a creative groove. It's a place or state of feeling jazzed, uninhibited, endorphins flying and all is clicking along with no conscious effort or self-doubt. I may have convinced myself of this state of happiness as pure crazed ability to tap into my natural talent. Many of us who do what we love have felt this, yet all is not perfect or permanent in stage two either. We must seek what is still higher.

> ***Stage 3: Ahhhh, spiritual happiness.*** When we want to know the self and are striving toward knowing it, our happiness increases proportionately. It is by determining who we are as well as the gift and higher purpose blessed upon us by the universe, God, or a higher guide that, at this point, we can begin to imagine that our happiness has unlimited potential perhaps out to infinity. Keep going forward as there are higher aspects of happiness yet to attain. It's time to go after that and enjoy your journey on the path to sustained happiness.

Sustained happiness is, in fact, a journey, not the next level of what you think it's supposed to be or look like. Looking within is part of the transformation process and is much like digging for gold. The gold itself is the happy zone in which you thrive. No matter how quickly change is occurring around us, be confident of your own happiness. Once you recognize that your gifts are to serve and your happiness paves the way, your financial life, home life, personal and love lives will flourish in surprising and fantastic ways.

CHAPTER 5

You are the Silver Lining

> "Being happy doesn't mean everything is perfect. It means you decided to look beyond the imperfections."
> – ARISTOTLE

AS YOU BEGIN YOUR NEW JOURNEY OF CREATING A life you desire, it is imperative to first become balanced. What does that mean?

For you to reach your true heart's desire requires a reconfiguring of what you're doing now. Whatever it is you're doing now has not gotten you closer to where you want to be, so it is essential to make some simple or possibly radical changes to your lifestyle and life story. For example, you may have wonderful family, friends, and a place where you are living, yet you desire MORE. You may have not felt fulfilled for a while. You want to move toward a new chapter in your life. For the new to come in, the old must be released. This might mean unloading the clutter in your life, the people who are not in alignment with your desires, and the habits you have developed that may be preventing you with clearing the obstacles on your path to change. However, setting new boundaries in combination with self-love is easier said than done. You cannot give when you are feeling unfulfilled within. You will suffer, as will your relationships.

Let's start with your personal habits. We all know that it never seems as if there are enough hours in a day. However, it's how you utilize those hours that really make the difference. First, recognize if you may be a workaholic who prevents an hour or two from spending more family time, exercise time, social time or "me" time. What can you do to cut back on one main factor that is taking up too much of your time that might add more balance to your life? Perhaps you are isolating yourself and not shaking up your routine, traveling in the same four corners of your world — same Starbucks, same drive through town, and same interactions with the same people. Or, you may be a giver or people pleaser and you give so much of yourself and your time to other people that your own life is placed on the back burner.

For those who have experienced a job loss, the loss of a friend, family member, spouse, or an unexpected occurrence, the loss represents a symbol of universal law. It is a change that was inevitable or unbeknownst to you, but the order of timing and alignment reached a point of calibration that has affected your life. The universe has taken you to the edge to where change is in order. How you react to this change is crucial to understanding what your options may be. The factors you have control over determine a level of direction from which you can choose unlike what you no longer have control over. The sooner you accept what you cannot control, the sooner you will move forward.

Feeling out of balance comes from an area of your life where something or everything may not be flowing as you had originally planned. This represents a time in which you made a decision in your life that did not align with what your soul intent meant. Your ego took over and ignored your soul's compass to guide you. Unfortunately, this happens to so many of us who ignore our soul's intent and no amount of money, power, or friends will lead to fulfillment.

Have you experienced days when it all is clicking along? You breezed through a good day of work, appointments and phone calls completed, errands checked off, fit in a quick exercise workout, had a good dinner and got a full night's sleep. That's not a bad day at all! In fact, it was a good day. The flow was present and you felt aligned as well as productive with overcoming any little bumps throughout the day.

However, balance in today's world is almost non-existent. The good news is you now have an opportunity for re-defining what success means to you. The new balance is about your new lifestyle, which encourages an intentional balance for what counts and matters most to you.

Reflection Questions: What are the key strengths that you can nurture and capitalize upon to redefine your success and take it to the next level?

_____

_____

_____

What area(s) of your life would you like to re-define?

_____

_____

_____

> Empowerment tip: "To live is to choose. But to choose well, you must know who you are and what you stand for, where you want to go and why you want to get there."
> – KOFI ANNAN

Your Soul's Intent

Imagine the cells of your being; inside those cells, your DNA is significantly crafted with talent, looks and perfection all wrapped into packages that have built your very makeup. This is where your responsibility for loving care of the very deep layer of self — your soul — is. In your heart are the answers and the messenger that your soul utilizes. It is your brain where logic may or may not decipher what your heart is telling you. You can go the route of robotic motion and the voice in your head that says "you should be doing this or that," Both yield resentment. Conversely, the heart path is that of freedom and passion, which is the natural and willing avenue linked directly to your soul zone.

Your soul has an original intent. At some point, you may have walked away from this intent or unforeseen circumstances have negated this intent. By turning to the soul portion of the book, it is now time to overcome your fear of self-expression and be who you are meant to be rather than what society, parents, friends, siblings, or corporate America dictates. Those types of projections are based on fear, not on love.

Whatever you chose as your next new dream project to reach your heart's desire, what would that entail and how would it look and feel like to you?

_____

_____

_____

TIP: Imagine the possibilities as being endless with no limitations or obstacles.

Lifestyle Steps for Reaching a New Balance

The techniques in your pursuit of happiness entail mindfulness. Popularized in the West by Jon Kabat-Zinn, Professor of Medicine Emeritus and founding director of the Stress Reduction Clinic and the Center for Mindfulness in Medicine, Health Care, and Society at the University of Massachusetts Medical School, mindfulness is the focusing of attention and awareness, based on the concept of mindfulness in Buddhist meditation. Research suggests that mindfulness practices are useful in the treatment of pain, stress, anxiety, depressive relapse, disordered eating, and addiction.

So what is mindfulness? Scott R. Bishop, Mark Lau, and colleagues offered a two-component model of mindfulness:

> *"The first component [of mindfulness] involves the self-regulation of attention so that it is maintained on immediate experience, thereby allowing for increased recognition of mental events in the present moment. The second component involves adopting a particular orientation toward one's experiences in the present moment, an orientation that is characterized by curiosity, openness, and acceptance."*

Mindfulness encourages an inner shift and prompts awareness for alignment to take place. As you continue to practice mindfulness, you will experience synchronistic occurrences; this is the universe answering your soul's intent. Below are a few techniques of which some may already be incorporated into your daily practice:

First, get out of your own way. Fear, greed, self-centeredness and the "what's in it for me" point of reference are components of an unfashionable 20th century mindset and not what the universe or your inner guide has in store. In fact, it's just the opposite. Tapping into self, calming your mind, and making sense of your feelings encourage authenticity while putting your ego at bay.

Second, meditation is a powerful exercise for learning to calm the mind. Your most creative ideas and "aha" moments emerge through meditation. Perhaps this is why long showers, a walk or running, or biking is so therapeutic. Alone time can be released and the engine of your essence can kick into gear.

Third, a belief mantra is an essential and powerful affirmation of self and the world around you. One that I often say to self is: "I am a powerful being and all my hopes and desires are happening in divine timing." A little self-assurance can go a long way, especially since patience is essential to permitting the change from within.

It is important to be content with where you are in the moment. Are you feeling good overall about where you are at this moment? Check in with self. How are you feeling? Are you paying attention to your intuition with what it is whispering to you?

Fourth, journaling is an excellent form of self-expression. Exercising the right side of the brain opens the door to your unconscious thoughts. As you lower your defense mechanisms, your feelings, brilliant ideas and leftover toxic emotions will surface. It's a gentle form of letting go while transforming toward those next life steps. A mind dump is so freeing to your soul!

Let go of resentments. Forgiveness is a form of acceptance. More importantly, forgive yourself.

Fifth, stop worrying. It is a useless energy zapper and increases stress. Take advantage of this energy and use it to make necessary changes for yourself. This will free you to blossom into your purpose and passion.

Sixth, practice a mantra that counteracts your worry, such as, "I am doing the best I can do for today."

Seventh, pamper yourself. We live in a society of go, go, go and distractions that veer you away from your dreams. Treat yourself kindly a little bit every day; it does not have to be expensive but make it something that encourages alignment. Try a bubble bath with some Hawaiian music and candles, a soothing cup of herbal tea, read a good book, enjoy a massage, time in the sunshine while listening to the waves lap against the shoreline, yoga and a good night's rest.

Eighth, clean house — Let go of what no longer serves you — from clutter and old papers to "so-called" friends who are draining and zapping your energy. Refresh your life and use your new energy toward what you want, not what everyone wants from you.

Lastly, practice JOY — Just Own Yourself. Listen to your body and your intuition, and act upon what feels right to you! Breathe in, think, ponder, and then decide. Operating out of fear, being in a hurry, or doing what others expect of you does not equate to your JOY. In fact, this is where our personal free will is tested and our ego tends to absorb this external energy, muffling our true feelings. It can be so much so that our joy is hindered and, over time, can become absent if not for consciously checking in on our higher self-known as our essence and intuition.

A New Perspective

The roles you were given as a child are often what you may still be carrying around, which may be one of the obstacles limiting you at this time. Perhaps it was your birth order, if you were the smart one in school, the artsy one, or the athlete. All have an effect on how you were perceived and treated, which influenced your self-esteem and behaviors as well as how you view and perceive the world. Your perspective is all relative and you have the power to change that quickly and effectively.

What role(s) have you carried with you since childhood (the parent-child, the baby, the lazy one, the scapegoat, the leader, the good girl, mama's boy, daddy's girl, the super athlete, the geek, etc.)?

_____

_____

_____

What expectations do you carry of yourself and others related to this role?

_____

_____

_____

Whatever deep-seeded perception(s) of yourself that you have, which is no longer working for you, it's now time to BREAK OUT, grow up from that inner child, and be who you are meant to be in all its full form and color:

> "Love is what we are born with. Fear is what we have learned here. The spiritual journey is the unlearning of fear and the acceptance of love back into our hearts."
> – MARIANNE WILLIAMSON

When you are ready to become clear, you will move faster in your transformation and start to break out of old ways of thinking and believing about yourself. You will instantly observe changes taking place all around you. It will be a simple intention based on your intuition and feelings. Although somewhat unconventional in nature to what you might believe, it's key to carry the positive aspects of yourself. Letting go of old beliefs and expectations related to past roles calls for a celebration. The untraditional process I am speaking to is this: Start to imagine the opposite of the role that you are carrying around.

Describe here how the NEW and SHINY Adult YOU looks like, feels like, and wants to be perceived as:

_____

_____

_____

_____

_____

_____

Write down the intention you have of yourself starting NOW and into the future: Use your imagination and be as specific and crystal clear as possible. For example, you may have decided to change your career. Decide on the "who, what, where and when". Determine your dream employer, dream environment, perks and exciting people you will meet.

_____

_____

_____

_____

_____

_____

TIP: When getting back to basics, is important that you use both your heart and your head.

Do We Require More than One Love? This is a Trick Question.

To feel whole and alive requires two types of love. The two loves we most require are love of self and love of life. Most of us think we love ourselves when we feel loved by another, which can be a pick-me-up for our self-esteem and self-respect. However, this is external love. Self-love can be defined in many ways; in most cases, it's accepting you for who you are both inside and out. It's also about feeling comfortable in your own skin by not defining yourself by a man, woman, title or status.

You can love yourself and not love your role in life, occupation, or path. In fact, taking smart risks to change your life is self-love. To continue to grow and thrive in life you must love yourself and grow to your full potential. We are more capable than we give ourselves credit, requiring both a love of self with growing to your full potential.

Self-limiting beliefs can take over and often can take over our entire being if we allow it. Since we are vibrational energy that is having a human experience, you were created in a perfect and unique way by the universe and God. If he brings you to it, he will bring you through it. When you face adversity with your health, finances, spiritual, professional and personal growth, this is a sign to make a change. Simply put, change your perspective and way of thinking. Love yourself more by believing in yourself. You can do it and are not alone on your path. This in itself changes your vibrational energy for the positive. Lingering in the same old, unproductive energy is not love of self. Instead, it is beating yourself up. This can be termed as your lower self and is ego-based. By learning to love yourself, you begin to set healthier boundaries and feel all around good about your thoughts, ideas, and capabilities, for the most part. Of course, you may be scared. This is good as feeling a little scared means you are stepping out of your comfort zone — you are growing. Congratulations, you are living for the positive.

Self-love, like anything in life, is a process. Have patience and enjoy the moments. Remember, life is about the journey not the destination.

> **Mantra:** "I am love and I show unconditional love."

A Healthy Happy Self = Healthy, Happy Relationships

> "Looking for someone to complete us, when we already are, is a misconception. When we feel complete, when we are happy with our 'self,' then we will naturally attract another who is a complement to our 'self.'"
> – OPRAH WINFREY

When you learn to love yourself, you are capable of loving another, unconditionally. The universe is like a mirror; the reflection is that of you. Often, when operating from fear, you will either attract exactly what you don't want or try and control what you think you do want.

Protecting your heart from past hurts is not uncommon nor is the ability to gain trust.

The process of learning to be a happier YOU is the ability to feel free where your fears are unleashed. There are no walls surrounding love. As you heal, the right people will enter your life at the right time and when you are ready.

To determine if a relationship you're experiencing is based on a healthy platform of character with you and another, here is a simple method in the toolbox to learn:

Life Enhancement Tip: Determining "Your Stuff"

Each person brings his or her own issues. No surprise. Understanding your issues makes you more conscious of your baggage and how you can best deal with them. The less conscious you are of your baggage, the bigger your circle will be, thus encouraging an imbalance of wellbeing into a relationship. If the two of you together are more consciously aware of your baggage and able to communicate this effectively, then the triangle will be smaller as both parties will understand each other's sensitivities. In addition, once you differentiate the things that are yours, you can better determine how to behave and treat your spouse and share your personal issue, so if it leaks into the relationship, it does not turn into an "our stuff" problem down the road.

When you are consciously responsible for your healing, you can be a healthier and whole individual and attract a mate who is healthy and whole as well. Two healthy, willing and whole people coming together make for a long-lasting and fulfilling relationship.

Credo: Having expectations sets you up for disappointment.

Interpretation: There is a difference between expectations and agreements.

Stuff...

Expectation may be looked upon as an assumption or unspoken promise with an unspoken result or outcome.

Many of us have unspoken expectations placed upon us as a parent, sibling, lover, employee, employer, friend, and neighbor.

Actions distinguish an expectation from an agreement. If you have not read, The Four Agreements, by Don Miguel Ruiz, I suggest you read it to take a deeper look into what motivates you in your relationships.

If you do not have an agreement or are unable to form one that sits well between you and another party, someone will end up frustrated, disappointed, upset, exhausted or all of the above.

Actions that are upheld by both parties keep your agreement intact. Just as an employer expects you to accomplish the duties of your job, you expect to be compensated for your accomplishments. If your employer stops paying you for your accomplishments, the agreement is broken.

This Leads to the Life Enhancement Technique Relationship Agreement Exercise:

Take out a piece of paper and make two columns. In the first column, write down the names of those with whom you have a bona fide agreement.

In the second column, write down the names of people you have expectations of (no verbal or written agreement in place).

Now, circle the names of all the people in both columns who are toxic (they cause discomfort in a physical, mental or emotional manner that breaks your spirit) in your life currently.

If you circled names in the agreement column, then you are no longer happy with the agreement and have allowed it to compromise you. Perhaps you believed the agreement felt right at the time, but it really is not serving you as you thought or hoped. This does not mean the person is not meant to be in your life; it's just that the terms of the agreement may need to be tweaked. Therefore, it's not the messenger with whom you have a problem; it's the message they are sending that irritates you.

The people you circled in your expectation column represent you or the person you circled as mirroring each other. You have attracted in another the same unconscious thought or behavior you are doing yourself. Perhaps this person is someone you have linked to an unresolved relationship (family member, former lover. etc.) who carried a deep need you expect in a current one.

For example, my client, Kelly, continuously exclaimed that she did not want to be in a "relationship." She would flirt and get to know men who had a strong interest in her, and when they got too close, she would run in the other direction. Paradoxically, she found herself falling in love with a man who acted and treated her in the same manner she was when becoming too close. She continued to see this man who was more emotionally unavailable than herself. Hence, there was the mirror effect. The realization that her expectations had not developed left her emotionally exhausted and disappointed. She believed that her unspoken expectation (love) would not pollute her authentic self. Her authentic self truly wanted a relationship with a sacred love, but her earthly self was full of fear by protecting her heart. She continued to hold onto a false agreement with herself (to not be in a relationship) yet remained in expectation that when she became close to another an automatic relationship with her unspoken expectations as part of it would be understood. This is a no win situation where one goes round and round. Be true to yourself and others by learning and sticking to your own agreements. Love yourself before you open your heart to another.

Unfulfilling Patterns

As adults, we may be very aware of what our patterns are, especially in regard to relationships. Often, our patterns are comfortable or signal attention of what is a false belief of love and the pattern is then repeated. The definition of insanity is repeating the same pattern in hopes of attaining a different result. Patterns can be dazzling, eye-catching and complementary as if you are a piece of upholstery fabric. Many patterns exist and a few may go unnoticed until you decide to take inventory and harness that beast of a pattern.

Toxic Feel-Good Patterns

It's easy to be in our comfort zone doing the day-to-day activities, but if you are not feeling fulfilled and making each day as exhilarating as possible, then you're not living — you just exist. This, in turn, can beat you down as well as cause stress, anxiety, depression, and a multitude of health and wellness issues. To create the life you deserve — and I emphasize the word, CREATE — you must be willing to take a closer look at your patterns. Often repeated patterns leave us in a "stuck" position. We all have been there all too many times.

However, becoming conscious (aware) of your patterns is an excellent start in learning to not go down those old paths. Granted, this may take several times to break out of, but you have the power to make proactive changes.

We enable a multitude of patterns in our tricky little subconscious minds that have our conscious minds believe what we think or do "feels good" or will make you "feel right" or superior or perhaps feel nothing at all. These illusions or beliefs look like this:

> Hanging on to anger, resentment, or bitterness as a crutch for avoiding or dealing with inner pain and fear
>
> Believing that a relationship with someone will "fix" or "fill" a void, yet all you do is complain about or find fault in them
>
> Continuing to stay in or repeat former behaviors from early adolescence
>
> Not taking accountability for your actions or responsibilities by blaming others as the cause of your inability to have things go your way or explain your demise
>
> Recycling people. Going back to old lovers, former connections, and supposed friends for your own self gain in order to fulfill a void with in you. This is part of your own selfishness and is not a harmonious way to determine what your void (pain) is really about
>
> Inability to be alone, but having a constant need for attention from men or women so as to feel "needed"
>
> Overindulging in alcohol, drugs, gambling, and the like. It may feel good to numb your inner pain, but this is a temporary fix. Your pain is not a permanent feeling; it is also temporary
>
> Settling as a form of sabotaging. Usually, it feels good or appears good at first until a shoe drops and an "uh-oh" takes place and you have a realization that you took on more than you anticipated or cared for. At this point, you may be in deep and start to believe this is the best it will be for you or that perhaps you do not deserve more than this.

Overcoming your patterns is part of growing and entails growing pains. As you begin to become more consciously aware of your patterns, people in your life will begin to fall away.

It's okay if you have sorrow, inner pain or the feeling of sadness; this is you letting go of what no longer serves you. As you, me, and the WE move toward reaching our highest and greatest good, there will be growing pains. These growing pains build strength, character and moxie. Your moxie is part of your essence. You can call upon your moxie to move you through your fears and become more aligned with your passion and purpose. It's your truth! WE are all teachers and students. The world needs your strength, talent, and essence to grow and reach our highest potential. No matter what you are experiencing, we appreciate you no matter what. As you learn valuable lessons, you soon will be helping others by teaching them. You are not alone and your happiness is right around the corner. There's more about essence in Chapter 4.

Let's move on the next tool in the box for breaking your patterns:

Life Enhancement Technique-
Un-pattern Your Patterns:

Now you have an opportunity to make proactive changes and create a new shift.

To do this entails three steps:

ACTION = Detachment
PATIENCE = Commitment
INTEGRITY = Promise

The art of detachment entails separating yourself from a secondary gain or external motivator that involves repeating a pattern. For example, perhaps you are uncomfortable with being alone so you repeat a pattern of going from one relationship to another, which gets you the attention you crave even though you are personally unfulfilled. The first step is to detach from the craving and obsessive need for attention. This need appears as a self-esteem booster but, in actuality, is a large void within for a lack of love with self and an inadequacy with understanding what love is; perhaps this is related to feelings of abandonment. A release and breaking the tie with the love object (the one you feel abandoned by) is an exercise for letting go of this connection emotionally, mentally, physically, and spiritually. Forgiveness is a good start. The exercise on releasing is described later in the book.

Once you process and complete the art of detachment, it's an exercise of patience to continue to commit to your change in patterns by making a promise to yourself with moving forward toward your higher self (your truth) and not fall into default mode. Keeping promises and raising your vibration to a higher level by living in your truth encourages self-respect and integrity. At some point, the energy suckers in your life will become clear and your gravitation toward new, healthy and uplifting experiences you encounter will take shape. From there, drama will fall away.

Where to Start Healing and Opening Your Heart

"If you want to reach a state of bliss, then go beyond your ego and the internal dialogue. Make a decision to relinquish the need to control, the need to be approved and the need to judge. Those are the three things the ego is doing all the time. It's very important to be aware of them every time they come up."
– DEEPAK CHOPRA

We all have self-doubt. It is one huge crutch many of us experience. Often, our egos camouflage insecurities and self-doubt to a point in which we start believing our fears are our reality. Yet, so many of us give credit and fault for this based on prior experience of others' judgment of you. There comes a time to grow up and let go of those who do not believe in you. When people express their negativity in pulling you down, it is often what is termed as a projection (an unconscious self-defense that is a reflection of themselves). Damaging messages form in our ego from the judgments of others. Generally speaking, many of us are guilty of doing the same to others, especially those closest to us. This is ego in full form. To stop judging yourself and others requires an acceptance of yourself and where you are in your life right now. This will then put a halt to judgmental behavior.

Nine out of 10 times, people are projecting their own insecurities and self-doubt upon you! DO NOT TAKE THIS PERSONALLY.

This is not a time for your dreams to be squashed by anyone. You deserve to own your dreams. The question is: Are you acting upon them?

Permission to Get Out of the Penalty Box

In some way or another, your heart was hurt or bruised. Perhaps it felt as if it was ripped out of your chest at the time. We don't always know an exact answer as to why a person who you loved, trusted, or cared for turned around and hurt you. In most cases, that person was hurting and not at peace with themselves in their own life. This by no means justifies a hurtful action, word, or injustice toward you. Yet, why is it the ones your closest to you hurt you the most? It's as if you are going about your life and the person closest to you took an immediate sharp left turn and you were left not knowing where they went and why they turned off without warning. The result is that you are then left alone with feelings of betrayal and rejection.

When we have been abandoned, a common feeling is a very deep fear that we will be alone and the ongoing fear that we will lose the love of someone close to us. The root of fear IS loss of love, which explains why the opposite feeling of fear is love. The very loss tends to make you feel like a victim. The self-doubt, resentment, anger, frustration and questioning of "what is wrong with me" goes round and round in your head until you have completely closed yourself off from the world in an attempt to protect your heart. It becomes a world of privacy where you are not vulnerable to others, your heart is protected, and you are wrapped tightly to protect you from any potential pain. Your feelings are kept in under lock and key for fear of feeling them or experiencing pain. The nosedive of self-esteem evolves and the undeserving nature with settling for crumbs prevails.

Emotional pain is uncomfortable and can turn into a fight or flight situation. You may become your own worst enemy or end up on (in) your own way through self-sabotage. Or, the opposite could happen where you run from the pain, end up in a vicious cycle, and then wonder why life is not cooperating. It then becomes a continuous hitting of the same walls of pain through what appears to be an exit but is really an entrance back to your original pain.

Feeling your pain is healthy; expressing your pain is healthy; and harboring it is damaging and leads to deep unhappiness, which may manifest into dis-EASE.

Often, when bottling up your feelings, you forget to express yourself or are so scared that if you do express yourself, you're not sure what might pour out of you and you fear becoming a puddle on the floor.

When you decide to choose to step out of the penalty box is when you have made your first step toward loving YOU. Self-forgiveness is a process and an important one, especially for the energy spent beating yourself up or the perpetual self-blame and blaming of the other party. All this energy can be turned around toward a softer and loving nature of forgiving yourself and saying, "I am not perfect. I am only human and I accept myself in this moment."

Choose to be the victor rather than the victim!

Transformation Toolbox

If you want to transform your life, believing in yourself is very important. Here are a few tools and techniques in which to do so:

1. Take accountability for your actions and responsibilities, first and foremost. Write out a commitment letter to yourself about what behaviors and actions no longer suit you. Hold yourself accountable and learn to ask what would your higher self do right now? (There's more about your higher self in the next chapter.)

2. Surround yourself with successful people or a group from which you can learn.

3. Designate a mentor, someone who has experienced and accomplished what you aspire to.

4. Ask for help. A leader is one who knows that he/she cannot do it alone. To become the next level of yourself does not mean you need to do this by yourself.

5. Create a vision board. Your vision board will crystallize to the map of where you plan on going and what you plan on reaching. Realize it's not always the destination but the process from which you will learn. The board is a physical meter that can distinguish ways to breakdown your milestones into chunks. Once you accomplish one chunk, you are only so few chunks away from your destination.

6. Place yourself in a positive environment that is peaceful and soothing. Go to a place where you can experience your creativity and inner peace (This may even entail moving to another state or country that your heart is pulled toward.).

7. Develop a state of Allow, a knowing that your vision will happen. Knowing is about a feeling of the inevitable. For example, perhaps your vision entails meeting the love of your life. You know this will happen because it is inevitable. There is no doubt that the

person you are searching for is also searching for you. This is already in the works; the rest is based upon timing, location and your clear intention.

8. Set an intention by writing down what it is you plan to accomplish. Once you set the intention, you have to put it out into the universe and begin acting on it through a deliberate and strategic manner. Most often, when you write down a goal or intention, it is more often to occur. The concreteness of placing pen to paper and writing out a specific thought is powerful and is retained in your subconscious in a powerful way.

9. Practice consciousness and awaken to being in the moment. Mindfulness techniques and meditation are very powerful ways to lighten your heaviness and constant monkey brain. Our brain needs to reset. Meditation allows for you to turn off the valve of constant thought and surround yourself with white light from head to toe. This is a soothing and healing process when done every day for 15 minutes. Once you filter out the clutter, you become clear in your decisions for work, relationships, home life, and health.

CHAPTER 6

Go Beyond Being the Fence Sitter of Your Life

> "Life is a series of natural and spontaneous changes. Don't resist them –
> that only creates sorrow. Let reality be reality."
> – LAO TSU

It All Happens for a Reason

Life is a series of changes. It's how you respond to the changes that determines the flow to all areas of your life. You can respond out of fear or you can respond with faith in knowing that everything that is occurring is for a reason, which, in turn, opens up a door to opportunities. When life throws you curve balls, often that is the universe asking you if you're growing.

Sometimes, we don't want to grow up or be the strong one, the caregiver, or the one left behind. So, choose not to be. Perhaps your power no longer resides in a former role. It's time to take on a new role in your life. Facing adversity means celebrating life by having gratitude for what you do have. This does not mean your adversity does not feel real and painful. You are human and, of course, it does.

Stress has affected more than 75 percent of Americans, which is to say whatever is happening, as a whole, is affecting people and causing physical, mental, emotional and spiritual debilitation, thus leading to unresolved pain. This can result in physical pain as well.

At times, it's our own strength that beats us down. For example, are you the type that:

- Does not delegate and chooses to be in control at all times?
- Is hesitant to surrender?
- Overworks to perfection?
- Goes until you hit the wall of exhaustion?
- Loses yourself in any of the following: a relationship, work, family or your own wallowing?

While the universe will take you to the edge if you are living on the edge, you are not Wonder Woman or Superman. However, if you are attempting to be, the universe will keep throwing more at you as you magnetize this powerful energy to take it all on. Until you cannot take it anymore, a "death" or transformation will occur, asking you for a change for your greater good. This interrupts the low vibration from which you are operating.

I received a phone call from Susan who was in a state of mental and emotional exhaustion. She had been taking sole care of her elderly mother with ongoing medical battles, nursing home debacles and no sibling support. In addition, she was balancing a full-time corporate job while uncovering the fact that her husband had been cheating in their marriage over the past year. Susan had "hit the wall," so to speak, and proceeded to file for a divorce. During our phone conversation, she felt it was best to move out of her home so she could move on. Although I could not blame her for wanting to move on, I felt compelled to encourage her not to move out as this was the only stable part of her life. Why give that up? Full of stress and anxiety, I talked Susan out of giving up her biggest and most stable asset, her home, and encouraged her to have her soon-to-be "ex" relocate.

In short, Susan did just that. We worked on making her dwelling her Zen and brought out all her inner treasures to make it a home where she looked forward to spending her time. Not only has Susan recovered from her losses (deaths), she also wrote a book about her lessons learned and transformed her life as an author and a speaker.

In summary, sometimes it takes what appears to be the more difficult route, which, in the end, gets you twice as far.

"When you have come to the edge of all the light that you know and are about to drop off into the darkness of the unknown, faith is knowing one of two things will happen: There will be something solid to stand on or you will be taught to fly."
– PATRICK OVERTON

Face Your Truth about Change

"If you don't like something, change it. If you can't change it, change your attitude. Don't complain."
– MAYA ANGELOU

Three Ways to Deal with Change

There are three ways to deal with change: act, accept or affect. Dealing with change has a lot to do with your growth level and personality type. If you are growing and graduating toward a personality that is ego-less, then you are better able to deal with your stress. If you look at the emotion change ladder, 60 percent of people are fence sitters, meaning they would prefer to take a wait-and-see approach. The 20 percent of people who are cynics usually feel secure where they are or feel there is a better approach, but they don't necessarily act on it outside of self-sabotage. The people who are not in arrested personality development and have grown to a level of being a champion are the other 20 percent who are excited about change. These folks tend to be non-competitive, support others and feel a sense of harmony, authenticity and transparency with a capacity to see the success of change for the greater good.

How does change affect you? Do you sit where the majority do as a fence sitter or are you the resistant type at first when it comes to hearing about change? We all have a point within the fabric of our personalities that has a default.

It's usually the initial feeling or gut reaction to a change that is our default factor. This initial reaction is about control and related to our egos. Albeit, these emotions are not pretty, and, as you know in our family and interpersonal relationships, we often know how someone we love will react to a change. My mother, for example, automatically goes into resistant mode any time the norm is interrupted. Knowing this about her helps me

Emotions with Change

Fencesitters 60 % Population	Emotions Cautious to make a change Wait and see attitude
Resisters 20% Population	Emotions Felt secure Anger Cynicism Sabotage
Champions 20% Population	Emotions Cooperative Excited See the Bigger Picture

to better relate and communicate with her about life changes and prevents anticipated upheaval. When you understand the emotional ladder of change for yourself and others in your life, a proactive approach can be best, not only to control stress, but it also to better relate with others in your life.

One of the more profound ways to measure our capacity for change is to be more present in our hearts, minds, and bodies. This involves awakening our whole selves to the present moment and deciphering change in a conscious manner. It means having the ability to see the big picture outside of our ego selves by being in tune with our higher selves. Our higher self is detached from the defenses of our personalities. The more awake to the present we become, the more conscious we are of our environment.

Are You a Fence Sitter When it Comes to Change?

Although our personalities are undeniable, it is important to not only understand how your personality handles stress, but to also determine how you can reach liberation through self-growth.

As Deepak Chopra explains in his book, Power, Freedom and Grace: Living from the Source of Lasting Happiness, you know you are free when you feel happy and at ease instead of fearful and anxious, when you accept being good enough as you are, when you surrender to the moment that the universe is on your side and when you have let go of resentments and grievances and choose to forgive.

This is a practice and, in order to do so, you must learn to understand the fixated areas of your personality to move and grow beyond the mechanical to a free flowing, more sensual and interconnected communication with intuition, inner truth, and clear perspective beyond the veils of illusions of the ego.

According to the Enneagram Institute, there are nine personality types:

- the Reformer
- the helper
- the achiever

- the individualist
- the Investigator
- the loyalist

- the Enthusiast
- the Challenger
- the Peacemaker

To determine your personality type, take the quick Enneagram assessment at *http://www.enneagraminstitute.com*.

When you are aware of what fixed personality traits exist, you begin to see what a truly free person looks and feels like. You also start to understand the state of liberation and acknowledge what life is like living in your essence and loving yourself first.

"It has been said that the unfolding of essence becomes the process of living. Life is no longer a string of disconnected experiences of pleasure and pain, but a flow, a stream of aliveness. One aspect manifests after another, one dimension after another, one capacity after another. There is a constant flow of understanding, insight, knowledge, and states of being." (Almaas, Essence, 178).

Going beyond characteristic fears and becoming healthier, you are acting on your desires and the magnificence of your essence, your higher self. As you begin to walk and live in your essence, your light surrounds you, creating a glow that attracts positivity.

You may have to circle back in your memory bank to a time prior to a broken heart, a friend who alienated you, that kid on the playground who called you names and did not know any better, the absent parent or bully sibling. This means getting past what were moments of self-doubt, low self-esteem, and search for validation from others when all you really need to know is you were perfect from the start. You began with your essence so to live the life you deserve you must first feel you deserve it.

> "You have to become very still and listen while your inner voice — the very essence of you — tells you who you are. You'll know you've found it when every cell in your body practically vibrates; when you're filled up by what you're doing instead of being drained by it."
> – OPRAH WINFREY

Life Enhancement Technique: Essence Qualities

Circle the Essence Qualities that represent you or write out the ones that are descriptive of you.

Capture your essence qualities and the fulfilling feeling of your uniqueness.

• Authentic	• Affectionate	• Artistic
• Athletic	• Creative	• Clever
• Enthusiastic	• Expressive	• Exuberant
• Feminine	• Funny	• Genuine
• Humorous	• Happy	• Intelligent
• Joyful	• Loving	• Magnificent
• Natural	• Giving	• Open minded
• Innovative	• Non-judgemental	• Sensual
• Spiritual	• Trustworthy	• Understanding
• Integrity	• Self-Respect	• Peaceful

Your essence qualities are the very core of your soul and creative self. Why is this so important? Often, as you shift and reinvent whom you are as you grow in life, what you create everyday leads to the sum of your life. No two people have the same combination of essence qualities; this is your uniqueness and the meaning behind your life purpose. It's an integral part of the deliberate creation process in defining your essence, capturing it every day, and sharing it authentically with belief in your core essence. As you create, you will attract who and when you will co-create with; it's part of the law of attraction. The more you practice your essence qualities, the more passionate your life will become and the closely you will become aligned with your destiny.

Differentiating Your Best Inner SELF to Attract a Kick-Butt Life

Simply put, I categorize the three selves that most of us wax and wane between. Often, you will find your three types of inner self are associated with a place where you decided an event in your life defined who you are. How you responded to this event often shapes an inner program from which you operate. Although this does not always occur on a regular basis, in certain instances you will be able to coin which self was programmed during childhood, adolescence and adulthood. For example, a low self-esteem could derive from a moment when you were bullied or picked on in school or perhaps your self-esteem took a nosedive after a divorce. Of course, it is usually the lesson learned that pushes our self to reach a higher level, yet, we are only human and not all of our feelings heal from a deep scar in record time. We all have been part of the walking wounded on this planet; not one of us has been left unscathed. However, it's the lessons learned that turn rejection into redirection. You become closer to determining what you desire once you determined what you don't want.

The importance of understanding why reaching our higher self is crucial is the understanding in which it corresponds to how we relate to others and build relationships. Naturally, we all have choices in terms of how we respond to a hurtful event, negative situation, or lack of kindness from others. Yet, something so hurtful can truly stay with you for a long time. When we are conscious of our choices, we have set a new ground rule. Yet, an eruption of a past hurt can surprisingly come about that sets off a memory alarm where old feelings resurface. Well, there are no coincidences. Did you mirror a current relation from a past occurrence that resurfaced? It can happen and it may also be a red flag for you to recognize your boundaries and the need for further healing or resolution of that lingering pattern.

Einstein once said, "Everything is energy and that's all there is to it. Match the frequency of the reality you want and you cannot help but get that reality. It can be no other way. This is not philosophy. This is physics." This holds true to how we see our self.

The three selves described below are the lower self, the middle self, and the higher self.

Lower Self – (Ego) your lower self circulates in a confined space where feelings of self-doubt, pettiness, paranoia, jealousy or insecurity prevail. There's a tendency to compare yourself to others or accuse others of what you believe is an injustice purposely created toward you, which obscures your perceptions with thoughts of yourself versus the world. Your lower self may say, "I will never be good enough" or I can do better than her/him." Your lower self is a battle you pick and tends to stay in to fight it out. This lower self can turn toward habits, such as gossiping about others, enacting relentless behaviors, obsessing or hanging onto grudges, swallowing your pain with excessive blocks of time toward a past time like gambling, drinking, smoking pot, watching porn, jumping from relationship to relationship, and not serving others (martyr behavior) but judging others.

Middle Self – (Social Ego) Your middle self is the functional and everyday self that goes to work and lives your life the best way yet feels unfulfilled and is bored by the monotonous routine of your life, which generates the same feelings that leave you with a lack of excitement. You are giving much of your power away toward unproductive thoughts and feelings, to people who are sucking the life out of you, or with hanging on to hopes for change but not making any change that entails leaps. Perhaps making small changes and retracting back to a comfort zone out of fear related to yesterday's feelings.

Your middle self can get stuck on habits that take up precious time and distract you from change, including shopping and spending on items you don't need or staying in a location, job, or relationship where you are not growing. The middle self is conscious of the unfulfilled feelings and often shares this but may not feel deserving or comfortable with the status quo. Basically, you are under-utilizing your personal power.

Higher Self – (Essence Self) your higher self is the CEO of your JOY (Just Own Yourself) and functions at an optimum high vibration within the world. In most cases, your higher self-lives outside of a comfort zone, is scared often yet operates in faith despite the uncertainty, and continuously has a cup of courage each day with belief in self. You are doing what you never did before so as to achieve the outcome of your heart's desire. Every day takes on a new meaning about what counts most, and the creative process is in full force prompted by realistic implementation. The higher self has mastered being the architect of destiny and the champion at handling change.

Manifesting what you desire occurs faster when you operate at a high vibration by operating in the higher self.

"Anything that annoys you is "for" teaching you patience. Anyone who abandons you is "for" teaching you how to stand up on your own two feet. Anything that angers you is "for" teaching you forgiveness and compassion. Anything that has power over you is "for" teaching you how to take your power back. Anything you hate is "for" teaching you unconditional love. Anything you fear is "for" teaching you courage to overcome your fear. Anything you can't control is "for" teaching you how to let go and trust the Universe."
- JACKSON KIDDARD

3

You Create What You *Believe*

CHAPTER 7

A New Belief System

The Invincible Belief in Self is the New Way of Thinking

Expressing your authentic self takes courage, moxie, love of self and a feeling of vulnerability. While this can be both invigorating and scary, moving away from your comfort zone is a clear sign that you are living. This is not the kind of living where you are operating from what you do or don't do, what your career is or is not, or what outside forces or addictions provide you with validation. It is, in fact, just the opposite.

The Latin term, *"tabula rasa,"* equates, in English to blank slate or erased slate. Your authentic self is about love of yourself and accepting you and all your imperfections. I bring this up the *tabula rosa* term as a point of reference to turn to in order to tap into your authentic self and optimize your vivid imagination to create the heart relationship, heart home, heart purpose, and heart self as your authentic self is about love of yourself and accepting you and all your imperfections. This process invigorates creativity. Your passions and love of your passions exude and embody from your soul and only you have a fingerprint on what this looks like. As a creative being, you have the power to express your creative energies. Now is the time to embark on this and surrender to be who you were born to be without hesitation or distractions.

Your Sexiest Organ - the Brain and Plasticity

According to neurologist Dr. Athena Staik, "Thanks to neuroscience and recent findings on the brain and relationships, we now know the brain has amazing capacities when it comes to consciousness, personal healing and change — all of which together amount to happiness." She goes on to say that you have the conscious ability to rewire your brain and transform your experience of life around you. It's a way of life that flows in creativity and outwardly manifests the beauty of the authentic being you are on the inside.

Once you pull back the curtain to your subconscious mind, your intuition will override your ego. Your desires, dreams, and true motivations come shining through. Your life is a canvas; your essence is your perfection; your authentic power is your brush; and courage is the color in which to express yourself, your talents, and your manifestation, as this is what the universe is awaiting. Those qualities in combination with your visual, kinetic, creative and analytical abilities encompass a light with your purpose to create, teach, train, coach, mentor and express by touching and leading the way for others. You are in charge of your destiny. As actor John Cleese expressed, "Creativity is the life force behind all that we do."

Think about the humble beginnings of one of the most creative geniuses of our century, Steve Jobs, who was a child given up for adoption and a college dropout with an aspiration for becoming enlightened at the early age of 19. He partnered with a buddy, Steve Wozniak, a computer nerd, and together embarked on a vision from their computer hobby. Little did they know the impact of a computer board's evolution in today's right-brained, intuitive and practical utility mindset. Apple Computers was near bankruptcy prior to re-hiring Steve Jobs to return to the helm to drive the company. In turn, he sent Apple soaring to heights beyond the average person's scope of vision.

This is an example of authentic power: aligning your soul and personality with timing. In authentic power, the neural pathways in your brain are open and active, bringing forth many choices and options to pick from. You know what works for you and why it works. You know you can trust your inner guidance and you're willing to act upon that guidance even if it seems illogical at the time. It also involves an awareness of your body, mind and spirit. I like to refer to this energy as your creative groove — that time when you are on fire with your ideas, your motives, and your synchronization with the universe in an outwardly manner that just clicks! It's when time passes by in what it is you do, that only you do, and that is the pulse of your passion. This is deliberate creation at its finest.

You are a Creative Genius – Not unlike Steve Jobs, the capacity for creativity and your genius lies in your desire to get out of your own way — or more like for your brain to get out of its own way. A study by Charles Limb (Public Library of Science One, Vol.3, 2008) suggested that creativity goes beyond self-expression and shows that the brain ramps up its sensorimotor processing in order to be in a creative state. The study concluded that there is no single creative area of the brain that enables creativity.

Limb noted that, through brain scans of musicians, "You see a strong and consistent pattern of activity throughout the brain that enables creativity," during improvisation versus a memorized scale or piece of music. Therefore, once you give your brain permission to spontaneously dive into the creative process, the possibility of what your brain can accomplish is infinite because the spontaneous process has no boundaries (particularly compared with a paint-by-numbers approach to creating).

Reinvention – Nowadays, we are in a constant state of reinvention. As so much is changing so quickly, to keep up the pace, we must be open to both small and large phases of self-reinvention.

Are you reinventing yourself and unsure of your natural abilities? Here is an exercise that can distinguish how you can look at your skills from a big picture perspective.

Life Enhancement Technique: Crystallize Your Uniqueness – Write out the top five occupations you ever did that you absolutely loved (include volunteer roles, acts of kindness, creative projects). As you reflect on this, think about the environment, the pace, the vigor, and the motion of your body and brain while involved in the process of those roles. When you are clear, jot them down.

_____

_____

_____

_____

Write the top five jobs you have done that were a struggle:

_____

_____

_____

Write two different columns: Column A and Column B. In Column A, write the skills or strengths gained from the jobs you loved. (leadership, time management, business acumen, people skills, Photoshop, etc.). For Column B, write out what you learned from doing those jobs (you struggled with resilience, competitiveness, tenacity, patience, courage, humbleness, etc.)

Column A	Column B
_____	_____
_____	_____
_____	_____

Interpretation: Column A describes skills that you will most likely be doing if you're not already, will be sought after, and will be well compensated for. Column B describes the characteristics that will get you there sooner.

Whatever you have done as a student of life, you continue to carry with you as a barometer to master and later teach to another in the future.

A very funny waiter named Tom had a dream and it was not waiting on tables. In fact, he resented and detested it as he felt many people who he came in contact with were miserable people. However, he was well compensated as a waiter, not because he was an exceptional waiter, but because he made the patrons laugh, which made him exceptional. During Tom's time off from work, he was an irritable person to be around, knowing he had to go back to work to wait on miserable people. I encouraged him to express his comedic self at an actors' hosting workshop. So, he did where he discovered this was his element, his voice and his talent, and his harmonious passion. When compared to others in the class, he was a natural. Several months had passed and, at our next visit, I noticed how light, airy, and spontaneous Tom was to be around.

He explained," I lost my bitterness since I started to create." "Create?" I asked." Yes," he exclaimed, "I started a production company with a co-worker and I am writing comedic movie scripts. We named our company, have an investor and a known producer who is mentoring us." Tom's first movie was a local hit and Tom is now in the process finishing his next super-hero comedy, which will be submitted to several film festivals. Now, we are cooking! Tom is following his passion and his dream by using his creative genius.

Although Tom is not making as much money with his dream, he is happy and living his passion out loud. Placing emphasis on his happiness versus his misery has reset his life in a positive new direction. His strength and passion for expressing his comedic nature is what he loves to do and, in turn, he started writing out his jokes. If not for his patience and resilience as well as understanding of human nature by serving to the general public, his writing would not be nearly as rich in content. In addition, his tenacity for his new craft is what feeds his soul. It is usually what you feed that gets nourishment. If you focus and feed your energy in the direction you want to go, you will flourish.

Do You Feel Deserving of Happiness? – Conversely, when you are sabotaging your essence, it's as if you are unworthy and will settle for crumbs. It does not matter why you feel this way, but it's more about how you can change it. Ridding the deep pit of rotten feelings about yourself is about letting go of the esteem; if you do not, then the gifts of the universe go unseen by your own blind spots.

Not forgiving yourself for past mistakes or actions can lead to a masochistic mindset. You succumb to cheap shots by others, bad behavior toward you, and self-serving people that take advantage of your nature to please simply due to your inability to say no and stand up for yourself. It's as if your voice and your opinions do not matter, which is a false belief. Your perception of yourself becomes that of unworthiness and you unconsciously set out the doormat for others to stomp on you. This only turns into a life of living in false belief of your own self-worth.

Do not settle, as you deserve the best that life has to offer! However, you need to truly believe that you are deserving of these things. Again, we are here to be happy, and we are on this earth to enjoy life rather than feel a prisoner of it. If you are having a difficult time forgiving others and yourself, this section offers two cleansing life enhancement techniques. Both are different, yet synchronistic, exercises to create the mind shift required to move forward on your path of desire. I suggest learning and practicing these techniques on a regular basis and daily as, over time, you will come to realize that you have healed what was necessary.

Life Enhancement Technique: Inner Peace

This is a four-step process: **Forgive, Release, Gratitude** and **Imagine.**

Forgive – Part of the process of forgiveness is to recognize who, what, and when. Denial of our feelings, especially anger, can be an inhibitor to recognizing what appears to be the obvious but, in actuality, may be an emotional obstacle related to what you have allowed all along. In other words, you may believe you are unable to forgive an ex when, in actuality, you are unable to forgive yourself for what you allowed to take place in the relationship. In addition, one of the more difficult issues related to forgiveness is when the loss of love has occurred, such as abandonment, betrayal, disloyalty, divorce, a sudden or untimely death or even a job loss.

The Kübler-Ross five stages of grief related to loss include:

1. *Denial* - "I feel fine. This can't be happening, not to me." Denial is usually only a temporary defense for the individual. This feeling is generally replaced with heightened awareness of possessions and individuals that will be left behind after death.

2. *Anger* - "Why me? It's not fair! How can this happen to me? Who is to blame?" Once in the second stage, the individual recognizes that denial cannot continue. Because of anger, the person is very difficult to care for due to misplaced feelings of rage and envy.

3. *Bargaining* - "I'll do anything for a few more years. I will give my life savings if ... The third stage involves the hope that the individual can somehow postpone or delay death. Usually, the negotiation for an extended life is made with a higher power in exchange for a reformed lifestyle. Psychologically, the individual is saying, "I understand I will die, but if I could just do something to buy more time..."

4. *Depression* - "I'm so sad, why bother with anything? I'm going to die soon so what's the point ... What's the point I miss my loved one, why go on?"

   During the fourth stage, the dying person begins to understand the certainty of death. Because of this, the individual may become silent, refuse visitors, and spend much of the time crying and grieving. This process allows the dying person to disconnect from things of love and affection. It is not recommended to attempt to cheer up an individual who is in this stage. It is an important time for grieving that must be processed.

5. *Acceptance* - "It's going to be okay. I can't fight it, I may as well prepare for it." In this last stage, individuals begin to come to terms with their mortality, that of a loved one, or other tragic event.

Everyone deals with loss and grief differently and not everyone goes through all five stages. However, if you are stuck in a particular stage that is inhibiting you from reaching closure and acceptance, perhaps the time is now to begin to release your pain.

Process 2: Release – Your anger, resentment, or bitterness may have become part of your persona on an unconscious level. To start feeling lighter and free, the following mantra can help relieve the pain whenever the object of your pain enters your mind. Say the mantra to yourself each time the object of your pain surfaces.

Mantra: "I release _____ to their/its higher and greater good." This offers the opportunity for letting go in a neutral manner with no harm to the object of your pain. You may have to say this in your mind a hundred times or more to let go; however, this will diminish over time. The diminishment of practicing the mantra is a sure sign that you are reaching acceptance.

Process 3: Task – Make a gratitude list about the person you are forgiving and releasing. Write out what you have learned and positively have gained from this person as well as all that you are grateful for related to the connection.

_____

_____

_____

Process 4: Imagine – Try to picture what your life will look like upon releasing the link of the object of your pain. Begin to visualize the burden taken off of your shoulders and starting anew.

"Beliefs have the power to create and the power to destroy. Human beings have the awesome ability to take any experience of their lives and create a meaning that disempowers them or one that can literally save their lives."
– TONY ROBBINS

To create the life you deserve, you must feel you are deserving of it.

Ralph Waldo Emerson once said, "Don't be too timid or squeamish about your actions. All of life is an experiment."

This is no time to be shy about who you are and what you want in your life. As you become clear on what your desires are, set your intention and open yourself to the universe. This is the time to get out of your own way and let the universe deliver. However, you must feel deserving and be open to receive.

Now, most say it's better to give than to receive, but if you are often giving, when are you open to receive? Many perceive receiving as selfish or they have difficulty receiving, giving, or both. When you are authentically open to express your gifts, there is no hesitation with giving and you are rewarded for your gifts in which you receive acknowledgement, appreciation, validation, love, compensation or other material rewards. You replenish your giving by receiving. This may work in some areas of your life but may not be working for you in one particular area of your life that you would like to change. The following Life Enhancement technique will encourage your ability to open your heart and understand this concept with a new perspective.

Deserving

Life Enhancement Technique: Orange You Deserving? – Imagine you are sitting at a table with four other people. Your higher power (God, the universe — whichever works for you best) hands you a bowl of oranges. There are four oranges in the bowl and five of you sitting at the table. What do you do with the bowl of oranges? Write down the first thing that comes to your mind.

_____

_____

_____

There is no right or wrong answer to this question. Whatever response you chose to do with the oranges is most likely how you give but not how you receive. Perhaps you are thinking how you might split up the oranges or just take one and pass the bowl. However, we are speaking about receiving as a reflection of your self-worth. To feel fully deserving, however, one must take the entire bowl of oranges for you. Period. You are replenishing yourself, which has nothing to do with who is around you or about sharing; it is about you, taking loving care of you, because you deserve it!

I was visiting with a very gifted writer one day who shared with me how upset she was with her current life situation. Sarah had financial worries where little business was coming in as well as financial disagreements with an ex-husband who owed her money. My feeling upon listening to her situation was how she succumbed to accepting this for far too long. She had traveled down a path where her light had gone dim and she felt alone in the dark. It was time to turn her light toward positivity and feed this path of growth for her to shine. She surrendered to believing that this is how it's going to be for her and was ready to spend her time in counseling to figure it all out.

I stopped her thought process and asked her to try the deserving orange bowl exercise with me before all else. She was willing and indulged in the process with nothing to lose.

About two months later, we touched base. She was the happiest I had heard in a while and had a wonderful holiday with friends and family, as well as more business than she could manage that came out of the blue. In addition, her ex and she had arrived at a financial agreement so she could put closure on this chapter. Sarah, who was once feeling powerless, took her power back. A new belief system had grown for her where she was now the architect to her destiny and no longer the victim of what she believed as truths.

The GOOD About When Bad Things Happen to Good People

My research about developing happiness and becoming the architect of your destiny led me to an inspirational woman, Haley, who is a living example of the power in believing in yourself. In fact, it was a life or death situation that brought her to a crossroads. Haley and her mom took a trip to India for a month, as Haley is an adventurous woman who is also a physical fitness aficionado. Her travels included riding an elephant, shopping for exotic treasures, and surrounding herself with the local Indian culture. Upon her departure to return to the United States, there was a bit of snag at airport security where her mother and she felt confident that it would be easily rectified. Quite the contrary occurred as Haley and her mom were taken in, handcuffed, and thrown in jail just a couple hours before their flight was to leave. To their dismay, an innocuous item that was thought to be a weapon was found in the bottom of Haley's backpack from a previous camping trip back at home, but it certainly was nothing more than a kid's BB gun. Nonetheless, the perception of the government of India was that Haley and her mom were terrorists. The unthinkable was taking place and it felt like a bad nightmare. Now, Haley and her mom were waiting in jail for a yet unscheduled hearing.

The conditions of the prison were, as you can imagine, small and dirty with no windows and barely any food. Heather was watching her mother wither away while both desperately missed their family and spouses. There was no contact with family, and their lives were dependent upon a small Indian attorney who did not offer much hope. Haley felt helpless, confused, and scared.

Once Haley accepted the situation she was in, she did what she does best by diving into her passions and strengths. Haley and her mom put together a team approach with the other cellmates to help one when the other was down, instilling hope, faith, and courage for everyone in the prison. During the outdoor breaks, they taught some exercise routines, knowing how movement is a therapeutic form of lifting us out of old energy and developing new and productive energy. While all this was taking place, Haley and her mom began to brainstorm on methods to get back home.

When you move your body, amazing things take place in your brain. Haley constructed methods on how body movements affect self-esteem, inner turmoil, and other physical and emotional breakthroughs by improving your body and body image.

In hindsight, the universe handed a bowl of rejection to Haley when she was expecting freedom. The experience changed her life and the lives of her mom and prisoners. In turn, Haley gave of herself and imbued her passions onto others. She was replenished by not only the incredible bonds made with the women in the prison, but she was also uplifted by the intense bond she made in terms of knowing how her deliberate belief in herself would get her through and essentially get her back home safely. Somehow, the universe was letting Haley know how kind, smart, and important she was to the world and how her gifts could be so magnificently shared. To date, Haley and her mom have been back in the United States the past three years and Haley now has a "Body Guide" and adventure business suited for women. She is in the process of writing a documentary about her and her mom's experience and their story of survival.

> "If you want to reach a goal, you must 'see the reaching' in your own mind before you actually arrive at your goal."
> – ZIG ZIGLER

CHAPTER 8

Happiness is an Action

> "The purpose of life is to live it, to taste experience to the utmost, to reach out eagerly and without fear for newer and richer experience."
> – ELEANOR ROOSEVELT

Hit the Defog Button on Your Happiness

We all have character strengths; it's a matter of recognizing them, polishing them and nurturing those strengths in areas that are beyond you. Perhaps you are bored with what life is looking like right now. We all get like that from time to time, but more often than not boredom is a sign of you not being challenged or useful; it's a sign that you are feeling unfulfilled. When you are idle and don't know what you want, the universe will send you unanticipated, unwanted situations which only confuse and distract you more. This makes it more difficult for you to determine what direction is right for you. It is not until you become fully aware and open your heart that your restlessness subsides and clarity kicks in. What this means is that you probably fell back to your default (old ego self) and allowed it to squash your higher self as a result of your fear, personal pain, denial, self-doubt, not good enough feelings or all of the above.

In Dr. Ellen Langer's book, entitled, "Mindfulness and the Power of Mindful Learning", she compares mindlessness to the unconscious and how costly living can be by living a life mindlessly. Dr. Langer explains how mindlessness comes about by default and not by design. In the traditional notion of the unconscious, we are not motivated to see certain things; to do so would be too painful. She states, "When we live our lives mindlessly, we don't see, hear, taste or experience much of what might turn lives verging on boredom into lives that are rich and exciting." By engaging in new activities, we move from living a mindless life to a life of meaning.

Start Here to Begin a Worthwhile Life

A new outlook toward balance is based on meaningfulness. You will feel more impact related to your goals and endeavors based on the feeling and intention you place behind each one. Organizing ahead of time and placing a positive intention behind each task and area in your life provide for an enhanced and meaningful outcome that makes each day much more fulfilling!

Develop intentional balance – Looking at balance does not mean spending equal time on all the areas of your life. That is next to impossible. Your job, health, family, exercise, faith, social life, hobby, friends, volunteering, etc. create a crowded pie of which we often bite off more than we can chew. This leads to burn out and causes you to feel overwhelmed.

When I worked in an in-patient psychiatric center, we had to write treatment plans for the patients we were treating. In most cases, we were limited to a 10-day treatment plan. This posed a challenge, but it was a platform to get people out of crisis and into the mainstream of living where the combination of coping skills, therapy, and medication allowed for a fast start to an upward spiral toward community life. When people followed a plan, they were, in most cases, successful. The same holds true for creating a life of meaning.

With that said, envision going in an upward spiral. It's like being on your favorite amusement park ride where your stomach feels nervous; you're excited and smiling from ear-to-ear, not wanting the ride to end. Capture this feeling and develop an exciting new plan for you over the next three, six, and nine months. Ready, set, GO!!!!

What is realistic and positive for you? Choose the top three areas of your life where you will plan an intention and spend the next three or six months on those areas?

Write them down (Example: three areas include home life, work life, and your passion).

_____

_____

_____

_____

_____

_____

What is the goal you plan to achieve for these three areas of your life and make them achievable, not pie-in-the-sky? (Example: I will move to a new home or create a home life that improves my quality of life; I will launch my new website and spend two hours every day gaining new business; I will write, paint, play music, and express my passion 30 minutes every other day.

_____

_____

_____

_____

_____

_____

What will your intentional goals look like and how will you feel about your near future? Will you be a changed person and how will you positively affect others? Example: My new home life looks and feels like, x, y and z, where I feel x, y and z; my new website has picked up several new inquiries that have created x amount of money; my creative project has led to x, y and z, all of which will improve upon the meaning in my life, such as...)

_____

_____

_____

_____

_____

_____

How to Stop Your Worrying

When you suffer from excessive worry, it tends to feed negativity, making it difficult to think clearly and see positive opportunities surrounding you. In addition, worrying can become a stressful habit that can keep you awake at night and cause additional havoc on your mind, body and soul. Cortisol is secreted in response to stress to restore homeostasis in your body. However, prolonged cortisol secretion (usually induced by chronic stress, fatigue, and, potentially, Cushing Syndrome) results in weakened immune, metabolic, and reproductive issues. In addition, a rise in blood pressure with links to appetite and obesity can be the result. It's obvious that stress can affect you in silent, but deadly, ways.

Strain is a form of placing blame. When you place blame on self, the situation, or others, you create more strain, which forms a victim role. Often, we allow one hiccup in our life to define our destiny. In most cases, the hiccups are what I call happy accidents. Instead, your future holds something much greater than what was in your past. Although painful as the hiccup or RUDEwakening may feel at the time, it is happening for you, not to you.

When my back pain debilitated me, I felt this was happening to me. The self-pity set in with a no way out kind of thinking. My whole body, mind, and soul were in a state of "NO, this is not happening to me!" By living in my "NO," I was not open to options or opportunities. My ego dug in her heels and stayed stuck in the mud and could not move in reverse or drive. What I failed to realize is that this one incident was shaping me toward a greater level, but it was an unfamiliar level. What appeared, as a barrier was truly a bridge to new heights. Transformation can be scary, exhilarating and exhausting. What feels as the "pow" and punch to the gut carries a message to your soul. For me, this was a message to find the one thing in life that set me free and, therefore, gain my happiness. To embody my happiness was to feel it, think it, do it and be it. This embodiment does not carry worry.

Instead of Edging God Out (EGO), an effective manner in which to surrender your worries is to release them. Although easier said than done, it can be done if you're willing. Your conscious mind is usually resistant and sometimes not trusting of what is out there for you, so you say NO. Saying YES to life gets you closer to your desires. By surrendering your conscious mind and its stubborn toxic merry-go-round of excessive worry, it's time to do the bait and switch.

Life Enhancement Technique for Worry

The God Box is a simple decorative box. However, it has miraculous psychological effect. I have experienced this personally as well as assisted countless people with creating a God Box and releasing what may very well be crippling them. Realize that this is just a baby step toward making change. The action you put behind your transformation is where the real results take hold. However, baby steps are still action and production that take you in a forward-thinking direction.

The HOW: Write down what your worries are on different slips of paper. With each slip that you are ready to release, place each slip into your God Box. God and the universe will assist in quieting these worries that are occupying your whole self and free your mind.

At some point, you may wish to extinguish your worries and tear up your slips of paper and flush them. It has been my experience that, you may review your worries and realize how silly some of them were and think about how much time and mental thought process were exuded because of it.

Rejection is Love Upside Down

We all have experienced rejection. Some events were more hurtful or painful than others. The bottom line is rejection does not define you; rather, it is an invitation to a new life destiny or perhaps a higher calling.

What rejection really means is redirection. For some, this may entail a new coping mechanism or way of thinking about self. For others, it could lead to a self-defeating existence where you feel you are not good enough and seem to believe you have to constantly configure, argue, or challenge your way through life. This is a defense to control and steer away from further rejection, which, unfortunately, seems to attract rather than deter rejection. The process of perceiving rejection appears and sounds like a circle of cerebral point/counter point chatter that is a battle of ego where you seem to get in your own way. The discontent you feel about yourself has been taken over by your power in which you need to be in constant control. This leads to a callous and lonely way of life where your heart is completely closed off and love has no possible way of entering nor does anything else.

Rejection is love upside down. Try these turn-it-around tips!

Claim your self-worth: The universe does not define your self-worth nor does your job, friends, spouse, parents, clients or co-workers. It is up to you to claim it! When you claim your power, you define your authenticity. This is no time to be shy. What you are seeking is also seeking you. Redirection often leads you to a new and much more fulfilling outcome that you may not have thought of otherwise.

Recognize what you do control: When bad things happen, we often react via flight-or-fight mode. Instead, try the two A's: to allow and to accept. This gives you the opportunity to process your feelings and ponder your desires proactively. We do not control the decisions, emotions, or personalities, of others. Let that go and place the focus on taking care of Y-O-U.

Detach: Often, we allow others to have too much power and essentially give our power away. Ask yourself, am I enabling a situation or being enabled? Enabling is disabling yourself. In most cases, the problem or issue becomes larger due to enabling. The art of detachment is a book in itself; however, the down and dirty way is to void your attachment of a feeling to the love object at hand. This does not mean you're being selfish; instead, you are replenishing your own soul. In essence, this allows you to go about being a fully-productive person in your own life. Often, it's when we detach that miraculous occurrences take place.

What appears as rejection is an invitation for you to start a new dream. Dreams change. My question is: are you dreaming big enough?

A New Type of Thinking and Living

All of us are fighting some kind of fight. You have all the strength to overcome whatever fight you're experiencing as a victor rather than victim. What do I mean by that? It's about self-image and the role where you have a different mindset. For example, when you change the way you see yourself with an image of victory, you will rise higher than the image of yourself right now. You may be financially struggling and looking at yourself as poor and incapable. Nothing could be further from the truth. You are a talented, smart, and abundant person who is fighting a financial struggle for right now. Remind yourself that you are a person of abundance, not lack. Perhaps you are struggling with a health or addiction issue and feel overcome by anxiety with a "no-way-out feeling." Don't allow for this to take over your life! Everything is temporary. What we see is always subject to change as nothing is permanent. You can choose to live in a negative cycle or you can learn the bigger lesson and change the way you see yourself and perceive your world. You have the power to turn your life around. Begin to see and create a bigger vision for your life.

For centuries, the psychological community has been trying to fix depressed and unhealthy people, but they have not paid much attention to the healthy, happy people of our society. However, Positive Psychology has reversed the focus toward improving "normal lives." The father of Positive Psychology, Martin Seligman, PhD., initiated a scientific intervention in terms of the thriving of individuals, families and communities. Positive psychology, as Seligman describes in his book entitled, "Positive Psychology: An Introduction" is a process to "to find and nurture genius and talent to make normal life more fulfilling, not simply to treat mental illness." The field is intended to complement, not to replace, traditional psychology.

Some of the major findings of Positive Psychology include:

- People are generally happy.
- Money doesn't necessarily buy well-being, but spending money on other people can make individuals happier.
- Some of the best ways to combat disappointments and setbacks include strong social relationships and character strengths.
- Work can be important to well-being, especially when people are able to engage in work that is purposeful and meaningful.
- While happiness is influenced by genetics, people can learn to be happier by developing optimism, gratitude and altruism.

Positive Psychologist researchers have segmented "happy lives" into three types: the Pleasant Life, the Good Life and the Meaningful Life.

The Pleasant Life is where you choose as much pleasure and positive emotion as possible along with the skills to accentuate those emotions. The drawback Pto this is it's not realistic to feel positive emotion 100 percent of the time. Furthermore, the positive activities chosen will eventually become boring.

The second segment is **The Good Life.** This is recognizing your highest strengths and re-crafting your life, using them in your friendships, love, parenting, work, etc. When you master this, you find yourself in the "flow" as Seligman states, or your zone, and feeling nothing while immersed in doing what you love.

Lastly, **The Meaningful Life** involves being consciously aware of your strengths and utilizing them by contributing and belonging to something bigger than yourself.

Dr. Seligman shares a few of his interventions that have been hugely successful in instilling happiness. The methods speak to specific kinds of happiness:

Have a Beautiful Day (The Pleasant Life):

Take a moment to design an amazing day for yourself. Plan out your entire schedule for one day that will maximize the amount of pleasure you experience and then live that day.

Plan a Gratitude Visit:

Write a 300-word testimonial to someone that has positively affected your life more than anyone else. Then, go visit that person and read it to them. Research has shown that even three months later, people who do this are much happier.

Strength Date (The Good Life):

When couples identify their highest strengths and then design an evening where both of them are able to use their respective strength, studies have shown that this greatly increases the strength of the relationship.

Fun vs. Philanthropy:

Have someone do something fun prior to doing something philanthropic. Whereas the happy effect of fun wears off quickly, the positive effects of philanthropy last. This juxtaposition results in extended happiness for the participant.

Based on Dr. Seligman's studies, he shares fairly surprising results regarding which of the three happy lives are most fulfilling and sustainable.

The Pleasant Life, or the pursuit of pleasure, has little to no effect on long-term happiness. The only time hedonism has an effect is when an individual already has the good and meaningful life so that the pleasure is just the icing on the cake.

Overall, the Good Life and the Meaningful Life both have extremely long-term positive effects on happiness.

The Power of Positive Psychology

If you are ready to change your course, you need to first embrace the notion that you are in charge.

Second, you must learn how the power of Positive Psychology should be a new foundation from which to learn and live. No one teaches this to you in school or even in life unless this school of thinking surrounded you growing up or through mentors.

To truly create a new paradigm and proactively shift from your old model, let's dig deeper into positive psychology to enhance your well-being.

In his book, "Flourish", Dr. Martin Seligman explains, "The goal of positive psychology in well-being theory is to increase the amount of flourishing in your own life and on the planet." This is in contrast to authentic happiness, more of which is related to increase the amount of happiness in your own life and the planet.

These are two seemingly similar, yet very different, perspectives: that of authentic happiness and Positive Psychology. What this tells me is that, to practice well-being, you also must determine what your flow in life is and align this with that of our planet. The type of mindset you need is to think for the greater good type of outlook rather than what is good for me is therefore good for you.

_____

_____

_____

_____

_____

_____

The key then is to remove ego and take on the Positive Psychology challenge.

Practice these three simple steps every day and see how your life changes for the better.

1. **Do what matters.** Doing what matters is important because you matter. When you do what matters, the action creates expansion toward greater fulfillment. By choosing temporary pleasure, you delay long-term happiness. Doing what matters my increase your discomfort, but this action is a sign you are on the right path of sustained well - being and fulfillment as part of your true calling.

2. **An attitude of gratitude.** Learning the lessons — even the painful ones — teaches us our own strengths. We tend to forget what we should be grateful for during times of transformation. Being happy with the important gifts that life offers us every day is a blessing. The air we breathe, sunshine, water, friendships and nature — the list goes on and on. When I journal about what I am grateful for, it opens my heart and I feel good about life. Try it!

3. **Trust.** Trust that everything happens in divine order. Practice patience with knowing that, whatever you desire, the plan is not always up to us, but it may morph into something even better than what you anticipated. As you open your heart to the possibilities, the universe usually delivers when your thoughts are free of limitations and you believe and trust in the unfolding of life. This is not to say that you are not practicing this, but perhaps there are untapped areas of yourself yet to transform and you are holding yourself back.

Perhaps doing what you perceive to be increasing your happiness is conversely, denying your own potential. It may be difficult to wrap your head around the practice of Positive Psychology when you are complacent. Complacency aside, you matter and the world requires your talent, abilities, and all the lessons you have learned, which can help others.

Create What You Believe

I'm not sure about you, but my creative muscle is being stretched and squeezed in all areas of my life now more so than ever. This brings me to the revelation of innovation defined as new things, ideas, or method of approach.

According to Daniel Pink, author of "A Whole New Mind, Where Right Brainers will Rule the World", our economy is leaving the Information Age and shifting into the Conceptual Age, a time where the creative types will reign. If you believe this to be true, then perhaps your needs and desires may begin to shift as well. Have they already? Perhaps even your feelings of what used to make you happy have shifted toward a more realistic or palatable perspective. So, what does all this mean?

Expanding what computers can do that humans no longer need to do has highlighted the areas where humans are irreplaceable. We know computers cannot generate beauty, stories, or moments and they cannot touch the soul that humans touch. Computers are a delivery process, not a feeling generator. So, just when you thought your right brain skills remain shelved, it's time to dust off your brushes, pens and nurturing side because you will just be getting started and appreciated for your creativity and uniqueness. However, there is a glitch. Creativity is just part of the formula of innovation or change. The key is to add in strategy, which is the why and the function behind the design. Once you figure out the why, you could be well on your way to a richer path where your happiness will be redefined and, of course, the abundance will follow.

The "AHA" Process Awaits

As your genius seed begins to grow, your intuition will be whispering to you to finish that project, redesign a function, or birth your idea into action now. You are already a winner just by starting! As you begin to make first steps with an innovative and kick-butt attitude, your goals will be different as well; hence, the method by which you were operating will then change.

A domino effect takes shape, not without a few mishaps or mistakes along the way, but no worries. Just tweak or change your goal, attitude, and/ or approach until it feels right and the results begin to take form. It's usually when you are in the middle of processing that your "AHA" moments occur. Part of living an abundant life is to incorporate play into your life. Many of us are void of this in our personal and professional lives. The process of play enriches those "AHA" moments and stirs the creative juices.

Think of ways you could add play to your work or personal life. Perhaps have a fun contest at work or with a project, do a field trip once a month, or simply go dancing. Whatever it is, make it different from what you have done before. Invite in the new so the old can be released. You may be surprised as to where a new path could lead.

When you are at play, amazing things occur with your brain!

What is Your Happiness Movement?

> "What is now your test, becomes your testimony."
> – JOEL OLSTEEN

You might be surprised to learn what really motivates you! Think of the one thing that irks you to no end, gets under your skin, and downright gets you pissed off. It is usually what you hate that forms an unconscious motivation to act with productive challenge, believe it or not. Now, hate is a really strong word and not one that is, well, positive. However, there is so much going on in the world around us that is not positive that it is no wonder there may be a few things that are unsettling for all of us. Let's be honest, we all have some type of hate toward something, which may not be expressed outwardly or on a regular basis. It is vital to your health and your life to express yourself. Some people do this in a reactive way while others choose to process, learn the lesson, and express it in a manner that I term productive challenge.

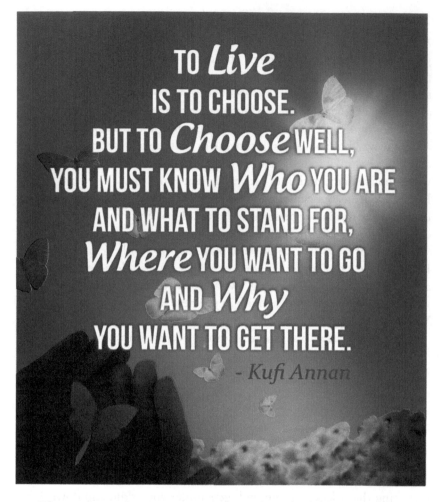

TO *Live* IS TO CHOOSE. BUT TO *Choose* WELL, YOU MUST KNOW *Who* YOU ARE AND WHAT TO STAND FOR, *Where* YOU WANT TO GO AND *Why* YOU WANT TO GET THERE.

- Kufi Annan

The media tends to sensationalize trends and celebrity nonsense and spend about one minute about the people affected by job loss, home loss, hunger, cancer, heart disease, depression, HIV, child and sex abuse, etc. We have all been touched by "something" where at one time or another, experienced hateful feelings. On a positive note, we become closer to what is really important in our lives and appreciate what we have by helping others. The surge toward collaborating with other entities, people, and causes is on the rise. It's a time for happiness, fulfillment, and positivity. Turning hate into productive energy is a great opportunity to share your voice, concerns, and care for others and turn it into a productive challenge. Your alias hate (aka, productive motivator) is your WHY.

The question is: What do you want to do that is great to change in the world and that is your personal vision? More importantly, what do you HATE? Write it down:

_____

_____

_____

An example of turning your hate into a movement is Darren Hardy's story, editor of *Success Magazine* and recent speaker and author of *The Compound Effect*. Darren came from humble beginnings and was brought up by a single dad with an unloving stepmother and her evil stepchildren. He was literally the redheaded stepchild that no one paid any attention to. As an adult and successful professional, he has come across multiple scams, faulty companies operating out of integrity and dishonest media hype. Darren's big hate is negativity. In his book, he discusses how to turn your hate into productivity.

You may not believe that what you hate could be the driving force to your occupation, endeavors, or life purpose. It doesn't seem to make sense, as we really want to seek and do what we love. This still holds true. Yet, your love has a veil over your hate. The universe is holding a space for you to share this message. It can be as simple as you may hate, hate, so your cause is about love. For example, I hate seeing people unhappy and not following their truth, so I developed an organization, the Get Happy Zone, for individuals and organizations to unearth their truth toward happiness and fulfillment. It is that simple.

What do you want your message to be? What do people come to you the most about?

_____

_____

_____

You are Great at ANY Age

> "Why fit in, when you were born to stand out."
> – DR. SEUSS

You can create a kick-butt life at any age. After all, age is just a number. No matter what stage in life you are in, whether you just graduated college, a new mom, in transition, re-building, reinventing, empty nesting or coming out of retirement, you have the capacity to express your uniqueness no matter how old you are. It is inspiring to learn the endeavors of all ages and to realize that it's never too late for your talent and offering to the world.

Just imagine how you can create an exceptional life, at any age!

Did you know that there are no walls between you and your dreams? There is opportunity for you to get busy and create what you believe or be an ingredient toward a happy accident as this is where creativity meets opportunity.

Age 102 – Australian Mini Munro marries a man younger than her, Dudley Reid, age 83.

Age 90 – Nelson Mandela is on the cover of Time magazine, featuring his "Eight Secrets of Leadership".

Age 80 – Jessica Tandy wins her first Oscar for Best Actress for her role in "Driving Miss Daisy".

Age 71 – Fashion icon Coco Chanel debuts the Chanel suit.

Age 64 – Louis Armstrong finishes his version of "Hello Dolly".

Age 52 – Leonardo da Vinci completes the Mona Lisa.

Age 49 – Julia Child writes her book "Mastering the Art of French Cooking".

Age 36 – Albert Einstein proclaims his general theory of relativity. The fields of astronomy and physics will never be the same

Age 25 – Charles Lindbergh becomes the first person to fly across the Atlantic Ocean in his famous plane, The Spirit of St. Louis.

Age 17 – Serena Williams is the first African-American tennis player to win a Grand Slam singles title since Arthur Ashe.

Age 13 – Bill Gates writes his first computer program.

Age 10 – Tatum O' Neal wins the Academy Award for Best Supporting Actress for her performance in "Paper Moon", co-starring her father, Ryan O'Neal

Adopted from the Great at Any Age gift book by Hallmark

Kick-Butt
Your
Life

CHAPTER 9

How Do You Operate in the Universe?

> "Just when the caterpillar thought the world was over, it became a butterfly."
> – DR. ROBIN SMITH

How Do You Operate in the Universe?

As we grow and evolve, our motivations tend to change. We all have a style or underlying force that drives us in a specific direction in life. If you have taken a ski or surf lesson, usually the first part of the lesson is to focus on where you want to go, point your eyes to a spot that you want to move toward, and not get distracted by looking elsewhere or you will lose your footing. Life is full of distractions, which is why it is so important to maintain laser focus upon your desire with the direction you want to go toward. The temptation of distraction can test your commitment level, values and self-accountability. For example, the most difficult, widespread problem among Americans is weight loss. The weight loss industry is extremely lucrative as food is easily accessible and solving our problems with overindulging with food is very common. People are motivated by results, how quickly they can attain them, and how eager they are to get to those results. Your method of going about this can often illustrate how you operate in the universe and how successful you can be with achieving your intended results.

In thinking about what motivates each of us, American sociologist, therapist, life coach and best-selling author Martha Beck offered her impressions about the four needs that drive motivation. We all have motivations which may stem from our subconsciousness and usually motivations can be subconscious. The four needs are *connection, security, accomplishment or influence.*

- If you often enjoy people and group activities as well as love to love, you fall into the connection need.
- The security need can be found in someone who prefers having financial stability and an organization to back them up; you gain strength from structure.
- Those who love to inspire and are born leaders have the need to influence.
- Lastly, if you crave competition and get involved in activities where there is a clear and measurable win, then you are highly motivated by accomplishment.

I believe the motivation style that you chose is based on either your old paradigm or one in which you find yourself gravitating towards. Your future lies in knowing that, wherever you place your motives and uniqueness, you will be most successful spiritually, mentally, emotionally and financially, if you follow your soul's calling. People gravitate to passion; people buy based on passion; and people exude passion as a way to touch others through educating, serving or assisting.

Have you ever heard the idiom "the apple does not fall far from the tree"? It means an apple carries traits inherited from the tree itself (i.e., carrying personality traits and resemblance, from parent to child, as well as the influence of family beliefs, both good, bad and indifferent that play a role in the formation of your identity). As one forges his or her ability to act on free will individualism and the control of others, his/her ideas do not have as much influence. Therefore, your true identity matures as you accept the truth about who you really are. In today's world, we are all linked as we raise our consciousness and rise above generational influences placed upon us. Across the generations, from Traditionalists, Baby Boomers, and Gen X and Y, personality traits, broader values, and behaviors are similar, but priorities are different. According to brickman.com, a research company, forming cohesiveness when social issues cause conflict is not insurmountable when addressing and leveraging each generation's strength as a way of bridging the gaps. But, being rigid in your thinking will have you believing the world is flat unless someone proves otherwise. Practicing compassion and a mindful effort constitutes a link to how we can better communicate. How we communicate is how we are linked. As humans, we have the highest, most sophisticated capacity to communicate. The ability to train or re-train our brains to link desires to the world we are living in today is essential, but a motivation mind shift in today's ever-changing world caused by moving from the Industrial Age to the Conceptual Age pertains to alignment with our internal desire and external world. However, what is most pertinent is how you communicate with your internal self. Your old paradigm communicates in such a manner that was working for you. Yet to graduate to a new, higher level of self requires a perspective beyond strength and more about stretching one's self based on the knowledge that your strengths will carry you through where a new form of communicating takes form.

So what's hot and what's not in the world we live in today and how we can reassess our motivations towards the greater good looks a little like this:

What's NOT	What's HOT
Industrial Age	Conceptual Age
ME	WE
Excess	Recycling
Materialism	Functional
Manufacturing	Organic
Trends	Sustainability
Corporate Greed	Innovation
Money	Gratitude
Competition	Collaboration
Industrialism	Creativity
Expectations	Agreements
Agenda	Transparency
5-Year Plan	Doing What Matters
Plastic Surgery	Anti-Aging
Balance	Well-Being
Fear	Love
Denial	Consciousness

As your positive transformation takes form, your unique qualities are also your greatest assets. As you seek the courage and confidence to transform your life in the direction meant for you, look no further than your own distinctive characteristics and behaviors.

Let's go one step further and determine your success style, which has more to do with how you navigate and operate in the universe in tandem with your dominant motivator. During my 24 years of studying human behavior and collaborating with some of the top thought leaders in the medical field, I have recognized three categories of success styles, all of which we use, although one in particular is your driving force to success and often what you attract into your life because of it. The three categories are: the Universal Leader, the Universal Creator and the Universal Connector.

Take the Become Fearless Quiz

See how you can become fearless, take the quiz at: *http://www.gethappyzone.com/take-a-quiz/.*

Check the characteristics under each that most often apply to you in your life right now. If you are having difficulty, then ask yourself yes, no, or not lately to each statement and only check the ones that are an absolute yes for you right now.

Strong desire to lead others
Ambitious about a mission or movement
Big picture thinker
Strong tendencies to inspire others
Unwavering belief in self
Analytic in nature
Strategic about making choices
Urgency to save people and change the world

Consumed by creative endeavors
Design and sequence focused
Visionary in nature
Prefer alone time
Learn by doing
Outcomes are predominantly organic
Vivid imagination
Perfection is a must

Incessantly on the phone
Remember numbers, addresses by memory
Constant urge to travel and meet people
One degree of separation globally
Think deep but communicate quickly
Get bored easily
Resourceful
Financial risk taker

- If you checked five or more in the first section, you operate in the universe as a Leader.
- If you checked five or more in the second section, you operate in the universe as a Creator.
- If you checked five or more in the third section, you operate in the universe as a Connector. If you do not have five in any section, choose the area that has the most checks.

You may have chosen five or more for two different sets of characteristics of which you could be a combination of Universal Leader/Connector, Connector/Creator, Creator/Leader or perhaps you were once a Creator and find you are now a Leader based on a new job, project, or position in your life. Perhaps you were downsized from a job and are branching out on your own.

Whatever the case, knowing your former core success factors can only take you so far; there is always a learning curve in earth school. This is where being the student can be fun and enlightening. In addition, you cannot do it all, which is where the other universal forces you can come to rely upon, co-create, and align to support your success.

For example, perhaps you are starting a business and find that you fall into the Universal Leader category. You may need to hire a Connector to get your business name and service out to the world or a Creator to design and build your website. This way, you can master what it is you do so well and let the masters of creating and connecting do that which they are successful. All three together creates a unified path of appreciation and fulfillment.

You can start having a kick-butt life by recognizing how you approach the world and who and what you need to collaborate with to build and structure your new dream and lifestyle. We all touch each other in some way. Your energy touches upon another who then touches upon yet another. Collectively, we all can create, learn, and excel at our passions and essence qualities, which lead to more people living in purpose and success. In part, the art to deliberately creating is aligning your desire with how you operate in the world that, in turn, attracts who or what is required for the outcome you desire.

Look how President Franklin Roosevelt responded to the Great Depression with the solution of the New Deal where the 3 R's were implemented: relief, recovery and reform. Relief was a response to the unemployed and the poor, recovery of the economy to normal levels, and reform of the financial system to prevent a double Depression. Many of the programs implemented in the 1930s exist today, including the Social Security system and the Securities and Exchange Commission, or SEC. For Roosevelt to be successful, it required a vision. The vision was then implemented and co-created by the Leaders, Creators, and Connectors of the 20th century.

So, you see how imperative it is for you to determine how you operate in the universe as you seek to express a talent, recipe, formula, method, technique, design, movement, operation, film, song or invention. Perhaps you seek the love of your life, a new home, parenthood OR reinvention of your body, career, home or even a complete life makeover.

The bottom line for creating the life you desire is to hit or reset the innovation button by moving beyond the familiar. Most of us did not start out being born leaders; you evolve leadership abilities by understanding the motivation of creativity. We all have the capacity to be creative in some way or form; it is how you choose to steer your attention. Evolving from where you are may entail doing the opposite of what you've been doing. There is risk involved yet following your heart is living in your truth. By not living in your truth, your soul slowly dies. That zest for life fades and the passion flame within is just a flicker.. We are all spiritual souls that are having a human experience. Your God-given talents are already within you and, because of that, you were programmed with your light toward success.

As we are all being stretched, mentally, emotionally, spiritually and intellectually, it is your light, uniqueness, and your ism's that drives what you are seeking but you may not yet be aware of this yet. What does that mean? It means that, no matter how you operate in the universe currently, you must always keep your eyes and ears open. The vibrations swirling about amongst us are especially heightened right now. We are all manifesting into newness while simultaneously expressing our desires with hope, faith, and intuition. Focus on this as someone may be asking for an opportunity and perhaps you are the answer to this.

Navigating global change by entering a new world causes a change within that affects your core. Author and shaman Michelle Karen shares her wisdom about how global change may be affecting us all on a deep soul level:

"Facts previously hidden may be revealed. We could completely reinvent the basis of our lives in such a way that it feels like we are reincarnating in the same body. Artists should experience a state of expanded creativity. Money becomes more solid and abundant for those who have been working from their hearts with great honesty to themselves and for the good of all. Self-destructive habits or patterns interfering with our growth are being exposed, giving us a chance to transform them. The veil between dimensions is thinning, allowing us access to secret, mysterious, subtle wisdom. Our relationships with our soul family are becoming stronger and clearer. The notion of time is both accelerating and collapsing. We could feel that everything is going faster and faster. Karmic lessons or rewards are appearing almost instantaneously. As we focus our minds and our hearts on new possibilities, miracles occur. We have clearly entered a time of co-creation where our dreams are giving birth to our new reality. More than ever do we need to think and act from a place of utmost integrity."

Sometimes, dreams change. You may be practicing the manifestation of your dream, but it's not happening for you. Give yourself more credit of your self-worth with solid belief and unwavering ability where failure is not an option. Or, simply open up your heart more as this will fine-tune your dream and allow for patience with yourself. Dreams can change and often do. Our lives do not always happen the way we think they will.

As John Lennon said, "Life is what happens while you're busy making other plans." However, to dispel this and transport your gorgeous self toward that big beautiful life that's in reach, you can dream something that is not yet visible and be able to translate your dream into reality. Thomas Edison, for example, had a vision and invented the light bulb as a result. The imagination is the root of all creation. Edison coined the phrase, "Genius is one percent inspiration and 99 percent perspiration." Creating something in the real world takes more than a vision and a dream. The challenge of testing your ideas and maintaining vigilance is paramount to turning your dream into reality. It took Edison more than 1,000 combinations of gas and filaments before the vision of the light bulb became reality. When you see something not yet visible, this sparks the creative imagination and sets the stage for work translating an internal vision into an external reality. Most give up before even starting.

What is termed as soul-centered vision can be described as the willingness to see a new vision; be in sync with body, mind, and soul, and imagine in new ways. When you are willing to see what is not yet visible, you can change your life or perhaps even the world.

With that said, consider what is within you, oozing to the forefront of your consciousness. What makes your heart sing and what do you enjoy creating?

_____

_____

_____

Write down the secret sauce to your passion with your special ingredient to what you do that includes your essence. Note: This could be as simple as your relationship talents or an edge to your knitting technique. My special signature is:

_____

_____

_____

Soul-Centered Vision Life Enhancement Technique
How to Manifest Your Soul-Centered Vision

The key to manifesting your vision is to surrender what you believe the outcome will be and instead focus on your faith in your goals and vision, and then get out of your own way. Many people become frustrated with why what they want to happen is not happening or why the law of attraction does not work for them. As I pointed out earlier, a few key ingredients for manifesting are in your life force. When you operate from full capacity with the ingredients you have, the obstacles will fall away.

The ingredients are:

Positive Thoughts – Positive thoughts create a mindset for attraction factor, which is the fuel to your life force. Your mind creates thoughts related to feelings. Often, it is difficult to turn off the stream of thoughts, especially if you are cerebral dominant versus heart dominant. An effective technique to use to relax the brain is to focus on your breathing as you would when meditating.

However, for this technique, simply envision a spout flowing water. Turn the spout to the left to stop the continuous flow of thoughts. When the spout is turned off, you can begin to, ahhh, breathe in the positive and breathe out any negative. Keep breathing in the positive and breathing out the negative, say this to yourself if it helps to relax, and sooth your feelings. The more you breathe in the positive, the sooner the feel-good feelings drift in. Good feelings attract a strong attraction ability and assist in manifesting the speed of your dreams.

Focus on feelings, such as:

Confidence	Clarity	Brilliance	Self-Belief	Fun Loving
Desire	Harmony	Faith	Greatness	Thrill
Love	Euphoria	Gratitude	Love to Self	Courage
Eagerness	Joy	Happiness	Inspiration	Exuberance
Faith	Excitement	Purpose	Fun	Well-Being

Faith – Faith is the foundation of hope, an assurance of things hoped for with conviction of things not seen. An unrelenting belief in self can be difficult when negativity, financial doom and gloom, and discord surround us externally. However, the focus within is where your belief in self is unwavering. Believing is absolute faith. Once you master belief in self, you are primed for greatness.

Imagination – Fast forward to a vision you desire. Hold the vision as a motion picture in your mind that has taken place. The faith with knowing this vision has already occurred becomes locked into your subconscious. Now, rewind and deliberately create and follow the steps toward what you envisioned with unwavering belief in the divine order of the process. Trust that your vision will slowly blossom into your reality. The trick is to emotionally detach from the outcome. As your vision blossoms, it may occur differently than the manner in which you believe it should. Expect the unexpected. How it happens is the journey. Enjoy the journey and practice patience as your vision comes to fruition because it will be worth it!

Now, relax into a comfortable space and turn on upbeat or relaxing music that settles your mind. Repeat the mantra: "I am love, I am happy,

I am whole." During this mantra, hold positive feelings with faith and begin to imagine the dream within. As you hold the image of your dream, lock it in, and seal it with a gratitude prayer to your Creator (Thank you, Creator, _____, for protecting me as you place me on my divine path.).

Your Supporters Are Your Board of Directors

Research tells us we are happier when we surround ourselves with positive people.

As you propel forward, think of who will sit on your Board of Directors. This is your support group – your connectors, creators and/or leaders. We all need positive people in our life to support us and lift us up. Write them down here:

_____

_____

_____

_____

_____

_____

"A man cannot be comfortable without his own approval."
– MARK TWAIN

CHAPTER 10

The Power Behind Your Kick-Butt Life

> "What we really want to do is what we are really meant to do. When we do what we are meant to do, money comes to us, doors open for us, we feel useful, and the work we do feels like play to us."
> – JULIA CAMERON, AUTHOR OF "THE ARTIST'S WAY".

THE POWER BEHIND A KICK-BUTT LIFE IS TWO-FOLD. It's making a commitment to your inspiration and placing action to your vision with a FIERCE vengeance! Have you uncovered your passion and determined where you want to take it? This is a process, but one in which the development of your personal revolution begins to take shape. A development of your personal revolution includes both major and minor changes in your personal life from health, wealth, love, wellness, family, as well as cleaning the corners of your emotional, spiritual, mental and physical areas of your life. Hence, you are now raising your vibration on a holistic level.

Much of this book up to this point has touched upon these areas. However, there are always remnants of cobwebs not yet whisked away that creep in from our unconscious that can alter progress or sabotage our efforts as we rise to our higher self.

When you are happy, you are clear. You are clear of what your intentions are and open enough to act on them with uninhibited passion.

What does that really mean though? Well, have you ever attempted to try something but seem to come up with excuses as to why you stop, don't see it through, or don't even try? You find every excuse from having no money, no time, or no one to help you or your inner critic kicks in as not being "good enough." You choose every obstacle as an excuse not to try. The analysis paralysis takes over and, the next thing you know, it's the holidays. Oh, where did the time go? A whole year has gone by and your passionate dream has collected dust. All too often this occurs. Don't allow another year to go by — your time is NOW!

Clearing the cobwebs from deep within is a pursuit worth doing because on the other side of your earthly self is a soul made of pure perfection and love. The answer to your true heart's desire is coming from your heart. Therefore, there are no mistakes to make. The only mistake is not taking the steps toward your true desires. So, before you sabotage yourself, let's dig deep into your conscious being and determine what is still nagging at you by completing the following exercise.

Clear the Cobwebs Life Enhancement Technique

Write on your Wall of Shame. Write down what you have never shared or been afraid to express and write it down on a piece of paper. Once complete, release all feelings of shame, sorrow, guilt, anger, sadness, and fault-finding related to the person(s), incident, or occurrence by shredding the paper into little pieces and throwing the pieces down the toilet (you may have to do this on several occasions when an issue arises so as to fully release the demons within). When you rip those demons to shreds, DO IT LIKE YOU MEAN IT — BE FIERCE AND UNAFRAID!

Why Living Your Dream Out Loud is the Answer

In my research of what authentic living entails, I found that it varied, depending on who you talked to and where you were in your life. When the question was posed to a forum of 50 artists and visionaries about what authentic living meant to them, the conversation hit several nerves but yet conveyed an honest, real explanation from most. In a nutshell, authentic living is about living and expressing your truth where the authentic self is the soul made visible.

Once you begin to place your heart-centered focus in all the areas of your life, you become aligned with your authentic power. It's putting it into action where most of us become stuck in our tracks. Most give up just before the miracle happens. Just the thought of giving up will have your old life calling you up and offering you a similar job and personality trait, that you so bravely walked away from. The universe has a way of creating distractions and testing your new set of values and self-worth.

So, what are you going to do about it?

How bad do you want it? You must want your desire so much that you are willing to make major or minor sacrifices.

Going Beyond Your Genetic Destiny

"You were born because you are going to be important for someone."
– ANONYMOUS

The power to go beyond your genetic destiny was depicted in the 2011 documentary movie, *"HAPPY."* The film makers interviewed people from a broad range of socio-economic lifestyles in different countries to find out what makes them happy. Research showed that 50 percent of our happiness level is genetic. Job, income, social status, age, health, make-up and materialism account for another 10 percent. Forty percent is determined by intentional behavior. This balance is the most influential factor in a happy life, the movie contended.

Therefore, 40 percent of your happiness is dependent upon your decision(s).

A survey conducted and reported by CNN Money in January 2011 found that 84 percent of people are unhappy in their jobs. More than a decade of research showed that happiness is directly correlated to productivity and morale. It is obvious that people are feeling unfulfilled in their occupations and perhaps denying the truth of their purpose or professional destiny known as the career you were born for based upon your natural gifts.

Defining Your Authentic Power

"Humbleness, forgiveness, clarity and love are the dynamics of freedom. They are the foundations of authentic power."
– GARY ZUKAV

Reflection Question: When do you feel most?

Everything you have learned up to this point has prepared you. Even if you think you're not ready, just start. There is a learning curve in anything new, but once you're learning, you're growing and this is part of living the dream.

The fear that is in your way is just a mirror of our own self-doubt. Fear is like worry, a waste of time. Stop entertaining your power on fear and start using your power by having a cup of courage and a little fun, dabbling in your dream and painting with your happy paint, which I describe below.

The sooner you start taking leaps of faith, the better you will feel. When you feel good, good things happen! When you think positively, positive things occur. Sometimes, you just have to let it all go, get messy, and have some fun with your passion. So get busy living!

Never, Ever Give Up!

Imagine your dream as a bowl of paint. Let's call your paint "happy" paint. You are the brush that dips into your happy paint and begins to make happy strokes within your current life canvas. The fun part is you get to choose the colors, the content, and the direction in which to manifest your dream canvas. It's okay if you make a few mistakes along the way. That's how you know you are on the right path to your dream. The magic behind all of this is based on movement. Movement accelerates into steps, steps into leaps, and leaps into accomplishments. Remember the things that happen to you do not define who you are. While you may feel like a victim, you can be the victor from the situation as every episode in life has a meaning. In most cases, it determines what you don't want so you can crystallize what you do want. What we learn from our past evolves us into our future. Are you moving toward your dream?

One inspiring story is about a washed-up golfer who, for nearly 20 years, was following his passion to be a professional golfer. He started at age 25 and won the Scottish Open at age 30, but he had never won a PGA tournament out of his 334 PGA starts. He was out there every day, pushing himself to be the pro he knew he could be. In the meantime, he was working side jobs to help support his wife and two kids and was unable to buy health insurance for his family. At age 52, he finally decided it was time to give up his dream and move on. However, all of his buddies got together and supported him for one year to follow his dream. They knew he had it in him. He was given a second chance to

DO NOT CONFORM ANY LONGER TO THE PATTERN OF THIS WORLD, BUT BE *Transformed* BY THE RENEWING OF YOUR MIND.

- ROMANS 12:2

pick up the sport again except this time around he realized he had to do something different to make his dream a reality. He practiced new mind exercises every day, hired a new swing coach, retained a sports psychologist and changed his exercise routine. He said, "It's better to be decisive than right." His attitude of perseverance and strong belief in self won him the prestigious senior PGA championship. In that one moment, Michael Allen went from "Michael Who?" to living his life's calling as a big moneymaker in his dream of playing golf for the first time in his life.

Increasingly, people I meet seem to be sharing the birth of their inner passion and are taking leaps of faith every day. I met with two gorgeous ladies recently, both of who have completely changed their life, livelihood and location. The huge leaps of faith are paying off and translating into happier and more exciting lives, doing what they love. There is no reason why you can't do the same. Yes, we all have to make a living, no doubt, and you will! Let's take a look at how you can make your dream a reality and be the architect of your destiny.

1. Don't leave your day job yet. Work at it but start your passion on the side or weekends. It may take a bit longer, but it will be worth it!
2. When you begin your passion, your mind and actions will expand where soon you will be doing your passion!
3. Birth your idea in some way or form. This could be a book, a workshop, a blog or partnership with an entity. All of these facets are areas that will begin the launch of your dream.

Your Vision is in Your Vibration: Life is Electrifying, The Mirror Effect to Our Lives.
The Steps to Manifesting a Champion Self

1. *Align* – Be careful what you ask for! Conscious Happiness is a state of consciousness that goes beyond your defense mechanisms and takes responsibility for who you are by living in joy and love instead of longing for it. What you think and feel is how you create your reality. Try taking a step back to look at the big picture with how your life movie has played out so far. What do you see? What obstacles in thought are blocking your path to freedom? Often, reaching peace is not so much about finding it as it is about observing your reactions and behaviors, staying present and whole with connection to the moment as to vibrantly engage in life.

You can manifest what you like through the speed of your emotional thought. This is part of a healing process. You will get closer to reaching your desires when you decide to hang up your insecurities and the need for external validation from others. Take the high road and accept you for you in all your imperfections and beautiful flaws as you move forward in your life. Give yourself a new title as the star and chief life officer in the direction of the greater good.

To manifest is to know and feel the inevitable. A large part of this process is when you release your emotional burdens, including feelings, energies, and people who are pulling you down. You become attuned to your body. The more you listen to your body, the more aligned you become. For example, there may be that really annoying pain in the ass person who shows up in your life at the most inconvenient times. Do you know who I am talking about? Your first thought is "Ugh!" You may feel that pit in your stomach and want to shove whatever responsibility or issue under the carpet. You may feel frustration, anger, or resentment related to this PITA (pain in the ass) person and a grey cloud starts to hover over your world. The opportunity here is to face up to why this person brings out these feelings in you. Perhaps there is something you are doing or not facing up to that needs to be confronted. Are you the one who is doing something, consciously or unconsciously, out of alignment and integrity? This is the time to face it, deal with it, and cleanse it from your life. A step toward growth means a step closer to your higher vibration where there are no more low-level energies pulling you down. When you are clear, your desires become crystal clear as well. In turn, your vibration to manifest a happy outcome is heard by the universe.

2. *Soul Centeredness* – When in a state of celebration, you do not perceive life or yourself through a right-or-wrong, black-or-white filter. Instead, see life as colorful by tapping into a feeling of freedom where life is electrifying! Think of your favorite amusement park ride as a kid. Remember the feeling and the butterflies in your stomach, laughing uncontrollably? You couldn't wait to get back on the same ride all over again. Capture this feeling and start manifesting your desire through this great celebratory expression. This is where your highest vibration emancipates you to new heights.

Whatever sparks your imagination currently is important to pay attention to, especially now. Use the inspiration you gain to take one step — or several — toward your dream; taking action to actually become closer to your happiness is better than no step at all.

Attaining your dream is a process much like the bud of a rose that is ready to bloom. Explore your feelings of faith, hope, and abundance, and you will blossom into a gorgeous flower. There is no room for failure or negativity in this beautiful process; failure does not exist. As you begin to blossom, your life will take on a whole new feeling and meaning. This can be an exciting time to not only fall in love with your life, but it is also an opportune time to love yourself in the process.

3. ***Being a Creator*** – The universe, with all its infinite wisdom, created all of us as Creators. From the moment you get up in the morning, the outfit you create to wear as your persona to the world, how you make your money, and live your life's work, you are focusing on or all parts of the creation process of creating. You have a lot of power as a creator.

Let's Talk about this Word, POWER

> "You are the power in your world! You get to have whatever you choose to think!"
> – LOUISE HAY

In today's world, POWER has been used and abused by organizations, companies, banks and self-entitled individuals. It's where the love of power has overtaken the power of love.

Don't allow anyone to beat you down! It is time to take back your power through the light of your own spirit. The power of your own spirit stems from your roots, your gut, and your strong belief of the scrappy, no-nonsense persona ingrained within you simultaneously. This may have been a persona you developed partially through genes and environment, where your knowledge in street smarts, ancient wisdom, an inner belief, family credo and whatever it might be for you that resembles a CAN DO spirit!

The "ain't no stopping me now" inner groove will have you stretching outside of your comfort zone in no time.

What fuels your power? Is it someone who inspires you, an action, or project that you accomplished or is it a movie, dance, book, song, animal, location, travel spot or an experience? Write down the first thing that comes to mind:

_____

_____

_____

List the characteristics of this inspiration that you admire and aspire to:

_____

_____

_____

You Are Enough!

> "Your greatest self has been waiting your whole life; don't make it wait any longer."
> – STEVE MARABOLI

As I ponder the concept of inspiration, it reminds me of where I grew up on the East Coast where, during a certain time of year, the caterpillars would fall like snow covering every area of sidewalk and driveway. It was difficult to play outside without skirting caterpillars along the way. I was mesmerized by the caterpillars' transformation in their chrysalises to become beautiful butterflies. Caterpillars do not hide in their chrysalises and, after a few days, poof, emerge with wings. On the contrary, inside the caterpillar are imaginary disks, which act as the transformer when metamorphosis begins. The caterpillar totally liquefies as the cells inside the chrysalis begin to regenerate themselves and the imaginary disks form wings, legs, antennae and organs. It's magical! How the caterpillar has mastered its metamorphosis entails a unique process unbeknown to humans, yet the magic is in the process. This precision encourages the caterpillar to do what it is powered and meant to do within the confines of its chrysalis. No fear and no reluctance, but pure trust in the uniqueness of its ability to create and transform.

While success is a process, usually a crooked line to achieve success is not read or talked about. Successful people are pondering and experiencing an unfolding process while figuring out who they are, what they know or don't know, and how to make a living and get paid for it. Therefore, progress to attaining success is not always in a straight line.

We often stop ourselves or believe that we are not enough. However, you are enough! Just as the caterpillar dissolves into a liquid, the success is in the edge and special power it possesses to transform into a butterfly.

As we re-discover our edge and determine new and next choices, remember you are in the middle of the chrysalis, not at the beginning.

In fact, you are more than halfway there. At this point, it is also time for you to make the next move and not wait for inspiration to hit you over the head. You may even have one wing partially outside of your chrysalis, but the comfort zone of your chrysalis has you frozen. Regardless of how overwhelming you may feel, think about what inspires you and focus on the characteristics of your edge and power.

You possess the one ingredient that no one else has. You are the key to a lock, the zest to a sauce, and the weaver of your own dream.

Steps to Kick Butt Your Life into Action

Change Your Life, Change Your Story

To create a kick-butt life requires a change in your story. We all have a story about who we are, where we are from, and what entails who we are today. As we are reinventing ourselves every day, so is our story.

As you develop your message to the world, what type of lifestyle do you desire to live in to go about messaging your cause, your mission your purpose, your vision or your kick-butt business or career?

To align your message with your lifestyle, visualizing what you want requires vivid imagination: think uninhibited, spontaneous, colorful images that are rich in content. Think about your essence qualities and go back and review them, meditate on your essence self, and very quickly circle the words that excite your essence self and which fulfill what you most desire your life to be.

Your Uniqueness is Your Pearls

Let's create your personal brand. Here's how: answer these questions with one word that represents YOU.

What you are now? _____

What do you want to be? _____

How do you prefer to feel or can you think of a word that captures your essence?

_____

Imagine these three words represent your tagline or brand image. How does this feel to you, play with it? And change it to your liking.

My NEW Lifestyle looks and feels like: (Example: You work less and earn more, do you want to travel, do retreats, speak, teach, volunteer, write, act, cultivate, invent, inspire etc.?)

_____

_____

_____

What you want to attract into your life is based on your imagination. This is yours and yours alone. Every moment is based on your extraordinary power. Embrace the power of your imagination! Whatever you are seeking, there is always a way — if you don't find it, CREATE IT!

Don't allow others to influence the power of your possibilities. Einstein said, **"Logic will get you from A to B, but your imagination will get you everywhere."**

Creativity is a large and often-overlooked force that illuminates your imagination. You can create anything into reality. You are a piece of what never fails because you have a divine capacity and ability to be what you want to be, as inner faith and belief are your new senses when you imagine.

Compassion is a force of unconditional love. It involves having no judgment of yourself, others and the world, in knowing that all is well. Judgment keeps you in fear while compassion keeps you in faith. As you move forward, focus on the compassionate side of you.

Enhancement Exercise for a New Life Style

Circle the traits that are closest to your dreamscape (how your dream looks and feels):

Serene, adventurous, fast, exciting, surreal, robust, balanced, free, full, exhilarating, complacent, safe, family-oriented, balanced or _____.

My new lifestyle is: community-based, home-based, bi-coastal, international, simple, rural, urban, open, city or _____.

At: the mountains, the ocean, a city, an island or _____

Located: in the West, Midwest, East, Northeast, Southeast, Europe, Asia, Australia, Africa, South America or _____.

Where I am a: trainer, speaker, educator, business professional, part-timer, information developer, designer, coach, mentor, salesperson, writer, and CEO of YOU, other or _____.

My message to those I serve is directed at: women, men, parents, singles, Professionals, CEOs, bloggers, single moms, seniors, caretakers, homeowners, small business or _____.

You disseminate your message by way of: social media, Internet, teleconferencing, workshops, webinars, and collaboration with leaders, creators, connectors and/or_____.

Your ONE amazing word that describes the feeling and aspiration of your Kick-Butt Life: _____!

The ONE amazing word that your IDEAL client FEELS about your business brand: _____!

The ONE amazing word that your IDEAL partner feels about you when you are together: _____!

The ONE amazing WORD that you feel when you are doing what you love: _____!

Gather all your amazing words and embody them within you, practice or emulate those feelings, and share them outwardly. WHY? It's the bucket of abundance within you that prevails.

The Fastest Way to Get What You Want

> If you want inspiration, BECOME inspired.
> If you want LOVE, show it!
> If you want happiness, SMILE and exude happiness.
> If you want respect, respect yourself.
> If you want abundance, be open to receive it and open your heart and mind.
> If you want money, serve others.

CHAPTER 11

The One Ingredient

WHAT IS MOST SPECIAL ABOUT CHILDREN IS THEIR ability to see and know the truth and not be afraid to say it out loud or express what we adults might be thinking. The art of not having a filter can be a blessing and a curse, funny or embarrassing, and hilarious or uncanny. We can learn from the innocence and truth that kids express. It's not because it is coming from the mouths of babes, but more with respect to the special way in which the world is perceived from a viewpoint untainted. The world is seen in amazement, curiosity, and concretely obscure. One way in which we can step back and appreciate who we are as people is through the perception that kids have of themselves.

Kids do say the darndest things. When asked what are your life goals are, here are a few that capture the refreshing mind set we as adults seem to forget:

"I am a girl. I have the POWER."

"Today, at recess, I will chase Annie and try to kiss her and I think I will like it!"

"I am a STAR! Because, I just AM."

"One of the things that makes me very special: My eyes, my face, my skin, I am GOD."

Do you remember, as a child, what you thought made you so special? Think back to the feeling of being invincible to life's obstacles because of your specialness. What made you so special and magical to the world that you were asked to join and be a part of it with your ONE ingredient that no one else has? List it here:

_____.

This is the ONE ingredient that makes YOU so AMAZING! Will you and when do you share this with the world? _____

_____.

What has been your lesson? _____

_____

What has been the blessing of your ONE ingredient? _____

_____

_____

_____.

How can you share your ONE ingredient to make yourself and others happy?

_____

_____

_____.

I remember visiting my grandmother's house every Sunday for spaghetti dinner. You could smell her spaghetti sauce a mile away and envision the hot Italian bread dipped in her sauce on the ride over. The whole family raved about the robust, the sauce — brilliantly muddy red, and piping hot, ladled over the heap of pasta and displayed before us every Sunday like a gift from heaven so magnificently made.

I always had a vague idea about what went into my grandmother's special spaghetti sauce, but did not appreciate the recipe until I was able to make it myself. One day, I asked her if she would share her recipe that was passed down from my great grandmother on the Italian side of the family. She showed me how to make it with the basic ingredients that I was well aware of until the sauce was almost finished cooking. Then AHA! My grandmother called me into the kitchen to add the ONE ingredient I was not expecting dashed into the sauce that added the pièce de résistance and generational signature at the tail end of the recipe. Whoever at the table ate this glorious and outstanding sauce every Sunday had no idea what set this sauce apart from all the others tasted in the variety of restaurants and neighborhood Italian haunts. Just knowing what this ONE ingredient was and when it was added made it special in and of itself.

When you share your ONE ingredient, at the right time in the right situation, is when work and life feel like play to you.

If you are holding back, the question is not so much as to why you're holding back but instead where did you get lost? _____
_____.

Get back on the path of where your ONE ingredient is shelved, and dust it off as your soul is waiting to kick some serious tail. When you do you will be living in your BLISS.

CHAPTER 12

Moxie Mantra Practice

> **I am well, and all is well in my world.**

WE HAVE THE CAPACITY TO RE-TRAIN OUR BRAINS. TO live within your light and shine as brightly as possible is easily achievable when you know how to peacefully speak to your soul and massage it toward the light. Here is a collection of mantras that you can use for various situations to keep you on the path to a Kick-Butt Life.

Mantras

> "Anytime you start a sentence with I am, you are creating what you are and attract this to you. So, if you sometimes say, 'I am bad at this, I am ugly, I am stupid,' these words take you farther and farther away from the part of you that is God. When you choose to say, 'I am happy, I am kind, I am perfect,' you help the light of God inside you to grow and shine."
> – WAYNE DYER

Career Mantras

I am a leader in my industry and craft. As an expert in _____, I am sought after by many and paid handsomely for my knowledge. In return, I help many people achieve their goals and exceed in their talents and desires.

I am a walking and talking goldmine in my field. I am a magnet for
  money and an inspiration to those who are a fan of my talents
  and trade.
I am the leader of my truth.
I exude exceptional knowledge and content.
I evoke my brilliance easily and effortlessly.
I walk in my wisdom with ease and grace.

Self-Compassion Mantras

I radiate health.
I radiate sex appeal.
I embody love and love surrounds me.
I feel gorgeous inside and out.
I am a vessel of love and light.
I exude femininity/masculinity.
I am powerful and strong.
I am perfect just as I am.
I embody a beautiful uniqueness.
I have an exceptional glow.
I feel good in all that I do.
I take steps to love myself and I manifest courage to be myself.
As I follow my heart, I share my unique perfection.

Life Timing Mantras

I am patient, as I know all things are occurring in divine order.
I feel the inevitable of my miracle-taking place before me.
I feel my efforts paying off as my seeds planted are now growing.
I trust the universe is on my side and God/universe is watching over me.
I know rejection is redirection with a positive outcome far beyond
  my imagination.
I am now on a path to newness and positivity.

Releasing Negative Energy Mantras

I release all obstacles in my path.
I release dishonest and greedy people in my life.
I release my ego thoughts about materialism.
I release ego thoughts that ripple selfishness and harmfulness toward
  others and myself.

I release my sorrow with faith in knowing there is a greater plan in store for me.

I release my pain and breathe easier today.

I release judgment of others and accept that their life paths are what is working for them.

I release my denial about my material excess and turn a corner toward greater awareness and freedom.

I release my denial about my co-dependencies and begin to walk in my power.

I release my toxic feelings toward family members and radiate loving thoughts their way.

I release _____ (person's name) to their greater good.

I release my negative thoughts and take my power back.

Trust Mantras

I feel centered in my life.

All is good in my world.

I have gratitude for the lessons I have learned and the blessings that came from those lessons.

I know in my heart I will always land on my feet.

No matter what, I continue to move forward.

Pro You Mantras

When I serve others, my gifts add value to the world and sustain me indefinitely.

I am a giver, I am beautiful, and great opportunities are right around the corner.

When I open my heart and act with love, I attract what my heart desires.

I am fearless and trust all will blossom, as it should.

I trust my faith to carry me through that which I cannot control.

What I believe, when I stay positive, is what I conceive.

Afterword

IF YOU'RE COMMITTED TO READING AND FOLLOWING the exercises offered in this book — even though you may not always agree with what I have to say — I guarantee it will have your subconscious mind bubbling and soon you will be acting upon your true heart's desire. Remember, you are the star of your life, act it, be it and shine brightly.

Regardless, perhaps this final question quoted from the movie, "The Bucket List", will encourage a new perspective of your life's path — "[to Edward, of the two questions asked of the dead by the gods at the entrance to heaven]: Have you found joy in your life? Has your life brought joy to others?"

It is my joy to serve you, in gratitude,

Jackie

About the Author

JACKIE RUKA IS AMERICA'S 'Happyologist', lifestyle expert and author. She founded GetHappyZone.com, an inspiration and well-being organization. Her mission is to teach people to be happier in all areas of life.

Jackie experienced a (literally) back-breaking accident when her car went off the road and almost collided into Buddha himself. She was forced to walk away from a six-figure career to save her own life, which set her on a profoundly personal journey to meet her authentic self and discover a true calling to inspire others.

Based on her own experience, Jackie guides people from the breakdowns that lead to breakthroughs, knowing the best opportunities are the ones we create consciously. She is a trained therapist specialized in verbal and non-verbal communication, as well as a more than 15-year career in healthcare, marketing and sales with moving Fortune 100 brands. Jackie has studied human behavior over the past 20+ years has more than 4,000 hours of client experience. Her background reflects launching personal and business brands with her specialized expertise in strategies and tactics, innovation and moxie. In this book, she guides you through the process of overcoming obstacles through her life-activating techniques.

Jackie paints her life canvas in Santa Barbara, CA.

Bibliography

SECTION 1

Well-Being: The Five Essential Elements, Tom Rath and Jim Harter PhD. Gallup Press. 2010

The How of Happiness: A Scientific Approach to Getting the Life You Want, Sonja Lyubomirsky, Penguin Press, 2008 (book)

Happiness: Unlocking the Mysteries of Psychological Wealth, Ed Diener and Robert Biswas-Diener, Blackwell Publishing Ltd, 2008 (book)

Happier: Learn the Secrets to Daily Joy and Lasting Fulfillment, Tal Ben-Shahar, McGraw-Hill, 2007 (book)

Thanks! How the New Science of Gratitude Can Make You Happier, Robert Emmons, Houghton Mifflin Company, 2007 (book)

Babyak, M. A., Blumenthal, J. A., Herman, S., Khatri, P., Doraiswamy, P. M., Moore, K. A., Craighead, W. E., Baldewicz, T. T., & Krishnan, K. R. (2000). *Exercise treatment for major depression: Maintenance of therapeutic benefit at 10 months.* Psychosomatic Medicine, Vol. 62. pp. 633-638.

Post, S. International Journal of Behavioral Medicine, vol 12: no 2, pp. 66-77. Keltner, D. Greater Good, Spring 2004: pp. 6-8. WebMD Medical News: "Hormone May Help Build Trust." WebMD Medical News: "Neglected Tots: Brain Hormones Lowered." Uvnas-Moberg, K. News in Physiological Sciences, February 1998; vol 13: pp. 22-25. Stephen G. Post, PhD, professor of bioethics, Case Western Reserve University School of Medicine. Gregory L. Fricchione, MD, associate professor of psychiatry, Harvard Medical School.

Stiglitz, Joseph, Sen, Amatya, Fitoussi, Jean-Paul; 2009 Report by the Commission on the Measurement of Economic Performance and Social Progress

Richard Easterlin "quote" Centre for Economic Performance, World Happiness Report 2012.

World Health Organization: Statistics Depression and Stress Amongst Americans 2011

Sharot, Tali, The Optimism Bias, Time, May 28, 2011

Todhunter, Colin, *"From Denmark to Bhutan: The Policies of Happiness"*. CounterCurrents.Org, Aug.18, 2012

Abdallah, Sarah, Michaelson, Juliet, Shah, Sagar,Stoll, Laura, Marks, Nic; Happy Planet Index Report 2012

Organization for Economic Cooperation and Development, Better Life Index, http://www.OECDbetterlifeindex.org

Sachs, Jeffrey D., Helliwell, John, Layard, Richard, *World Happiness Report*, 2012. pg. 48 & 49.

Handley, Meg; *"Americans are the Wealthiest but not the Happiest"*, U.S. News May 22, 2012

Koch, Wendy, *"Is the USA Moving Toward a 'Happiness Index'"*, USA TODAY, Aug.1, 2012

Thompson, Derek. : *The New Economics of Happiness"*, The Atlantic, May 23, 2012

Kataria, Madan Dr., Laughter Yoga originator. *Inner Spirit Laughter* Downloadable book. http://www.laughteryoga.org/english/diary/detail_view/36

Robert F. Kennedy Address, University of Kansas, Lawrence, Kansas, March 18, 1968

SECTION 2

Ryan, Richard Dr., Kasser, Timothy Dr., *A Dark Side of the American Dream: correlates as financial success as a central life aspiration.* Journal Of Personality and Social Psychology, 1993.

Stages of Group Development Theories and Applications of Educational Psychology, Bruce Tuckman. Wadsworth, 1972

Scott R. Bishop, Mark Lau, Shauna Shapiro, Linda Carlson, Nicole D. Anderson, James Carmody, Zindel V. Segal, Susan Abbey, Michael Speca, Drew Velting & Gerald Devins (2004). *"Mindfulness: A Proposed Operational Definition"*. Clinical Psychology: Science & Practice 11 (3): 230–241

Enneagram Institute Guide; http://www.enneagraminstitute.com/

SECTION 3

The Vibrational Universe, Kenneth James Michael Maclean, Loving Healing Press, 2006. (book)

Limb, CJ, Braun AR (2008) *Neural Substrates of Spontaneous Musical Performance: An fMRI Study of Jazz Improvisation.* PloS One, 3 (2) e1679

Langer, Ellen J, *The Power of Mindful Learning,* Perseus Books. 1997 (book)

Seligman, Martin Ph.D., *Authentic Happiness; Using the New Positive Psychology to Realize Your Potential for Lasting Fulfillment.* New York: Free press. 2002

Seligman, Martin Ph.D., *Flourish: A Visionary New Understanding of Happiness and Well -Being.* New York: Free Press.2011

Seligman, Martin Ph.D. and Csikszentmihaly, Mihaly, *Positive Psychology and Introduction;* Abstract, American Psychologist: Millenial issue Jan. 2000.

Pink, Daniel, *A Whole New Mind,* Why Right-Brainers Will Rule the Future. Penguin Books. 2005.

Hardy, Darren, *The Compound Effect.* Vanguard Press. 2010

Great at Any Age, Who Did What from Age 1 – 100, Hallmark Cards, Inc.

SECTION 4

Martha Beck, http://www.oprah.com/spirit/How-to-Determine-What-Motivates-You-Motivation-Style, October 11, 2011.

Michelle, Karèn, http://www.michellekaren.com/store/index.php?main_page=page&id=2

Michele, Karèn, *Astrology for Enlightment,* Atria Books/Simon and Schuster, 2008.

Belic, Roko, '*The Search for Happiness*", Huffington Post Blog, Jan.20, 2012

CNN Money Magazine, 2011, American's Unhealthy and Unhappy in their Current Jobs

Index

CPSIA information can be obtained at www.ICGtesting.com
Printed in the USA
BVOW10s1751300714

360975BV00004B/4/P